Seed
TIME

SELECTED POEMS I

Seed TIME

SELECTED POEMS I

KOFI ANYIDOHO

DAkpabli

SEEDTIME: SELECTED POEMS I

ISBN: 97899889022 3 0

Editorial Team

Martin Egblewogbe

Kofi Akpabli

Cover Design and Book Layout by

Nene Buer Boyetey

P O Box NM 78, Nima, Accra, Ghana

Email: bigglesmultimedia@gmail.com

Tel: +233 302 333 502 | +233 244 634 204

Published by

DAkpabli & Associates

P O Box 7465, Accra North, Accra, Ghana

Tel: +233 264 339 066 | +233 244 704 250 | +233 247 896 375

Email: info@dakpabli.com

In memory of Abotsi Korbli Anyidoho, Kodzo Ahiago Domegbe, Edo Kligu Yortuwor, Abla Adidi Anyidoho, Agbodzi Yortuwor, Kodzovi Anyidoho, and all the Ancestral Voices who prepared the field for our SeedTime.

TABLE OF CONTENTS

FirstFruits:

- My Song
- Agbayiza
- The Song of a Twin Brother
- Agbenɔxevi
- A Dirge for Our Birth
- Go Tell Jesus
- Brain Surgery
- Shattered Dreams
- Fire

AUTHOR'S NOTES

SeedTme brings together Selected Poems from my first five collections, beginning in reverse order with poems from *AncestralLogic & CaribbeanBlues* (1993), *A Harvest of Our Dreams* (1984), *EarthChild* (1985), *Elegy for the Revolution* (1978), and *BrainSurgery (*1985). *BrainSurgery*, the earliest of these collections, was never published as a collection until it came out together with *EarthChild* (Woeli Publishing Services, 1985), even though several of the poems had appeared in various journals, magazines and anthologies. The title poem "BrainSurgery" first appeared in *African Arts* (University of California, Los Angeles) and "The Song of a Twin Brother" was first published in *Okike*, edited by Chinua Achebe, and later appeared in various other anthologies, including *Rhythms of Creation*, ed. Donatus Nwoga (Enugu: Fourth Dimension Press, 1982), *Penguin Anthology of Modern African Poetry*, eds. Gerald Moore and Ulli Beier. *Elegy for the Revolution* was my very first published collection, put out in 1978 by the Greenfield Review Press, thanks to Joseph Bruchac of Greenfield Center in Up-State New York, who also published three of Kofi Awoonor's collections: *Ride Me, Memory* (1973), *The House by the Sea* (1978) and *Until the Morning After(1985)*. Special thanks also to Mrs. Margaret Watts, my former lecturer in the English Department at Legon, who forwarded the manuscript to Joseph Bruchac, a former Peace Corps teacher in Keta in the Volta Region of Ghana. *Elegy for the Revolution* was later republished together with *A Harvest our Dreams* by Heinemann in the African Writers Series in 1984, closely followed a year later by *EarthChild*, published by Woeli, released together with a Ghana edition of *A Harvest of Our Dreams*, through a special arrangement with Heinemann. The publication seven years or so later of *AncestralLogic & CaribbeanBlues* (Africa World

Press, 1992), seemed to have brought my career in the service of poetry to an initial/temporary closure.

I found myself drawn more and more into what was seen as my core business as a university teacher, researcher and scholar. It was a period of constant restlessness as I wrote conference paper after conference paper, journal article after journal article, even as I paid due attention to the large number of courses I had to teach, with so many colleagues gone to seek "greener pastures" in more rewarding parts of the globe. That was how come I came quite close to committing suicide as an active, productive poet. A full decade passed before I could scrape together enough poems for a new but modest collection.

Somehow, though, the sacrifice paid off, in its own pompous kind of way, as I moved from lecturer to senior lecturer to associate professor to professor in a relatively short period, mainly on the basis of my work as a scholar, not as a poet. Indeed, as I eventually found out, when I submitted my publications for consideration as an associate professor, my dean removed all my creative work from the package before sending it out to the external assessors. Why? They did not constitute contribution to scholarship!

Sadly, this kind of devious academic bias against creative excellence in such disciplines as poetry, music, dance, and drama, is still a cherished tradition in our institutions of "higher learning". There are many very learned colleagues, not only in the sciences but also in the humanities and social sciences, who are convinced that the creative artists are really "a bunch of jokers". So my books of poetry, Atukwei Okai's books of poetry, Ama Ata Aidoo's novels, books of poetry and short stories, or Mohammed Ben Abdallah's plays, regularly performed on stage and also published, Efua Sutherland's several plays in Akan and English, even Ayi Kwei Armah's several richly-layered novels with a profound sense and knowledge of history, and more currently Mawuli Adjei's novels, short story and poetry collections, etc., could not and must not count as serious contributions to scholarship, even though they are studied in many courses, at the undergraduate and graduate levels and are the subjects of various research projects, including Masters and Doctoral theses in Ghana and around the world. Above all, they bring some delight and deeper understanding of life to countless readers worldwide. But a colleague who manages to write a short review of any of our work or especially a conference paper or refereed journal article on the said work, has clearly made a profound contribution to scholarship, to knowledge.

Fortunately, though, the creative impulse is something of an incurable gift. Whether appreciated and rewarded or ignored and vilified, it does not easily disappear or despair. That is why I will always regret the many more poems I could have written but never did because I was too busy writing academic papers. It is why I am relieved that no matter how long my occupation as a scholar takes me away to conferences and peer reviewed journals, I will always come back to my preoccupation as a poet, as a singer. You cannot take song away from the singer or the singer away from song.

So it was special joy to return to poetry in *PraiseSong for TheLand* more than a decade after *AncestralLogic & CaribbeanBlues*, followed in 2011 by *The Place We Call Home*, and *Selected Poems* in Korean Translation, somewhat unhappily titled *Africa, the Sad Tropical Continent* by the translator Dr. Lee Seok Ho. (Kookhak Publishers, Seoul, 2012). And now *SeedTime*, which is planned to be closely followed by *See What They've Done to Our SunRise: new poems from an old loom*. As with the last two published collections, *SeedTime* is expected to be released with companion CD recordings of the poems.

In fact, the recording and digital mastering was completed more than ten years ago in Iowa, when I had expected the selected poems to be published by Ayebia Clarke. Unforeseen challenges interrupted and derailed those initial publication plans. My special gratitude to *DAkpabli & Associates* for the offer to publish these selected poems now, after such a long wait.

It is important also to note that several of the poems in *SeedTime* have appeared in translation into various languages: Bengali, Chinese, Dutch, French, Italian, Korean, Portuguese, Spanish, Slavic, Swedish, Turkish. The occasion for some of these translations have been international poetry festivals in which I have participated over the years, beginning in 1975 with the Struga Poetry Festival in Macedonia, Yugoslavia, and others, such as Medellin International Poetry Festival, Rotterdam International Poetry Festival, Oslo International Poetry Festival, Instanbulensis International Poetry Festival in Turkey.

A particularly important note on which to conclude my Author's Notes is the significance of the poetry and other work I have so far written in my First Language, my Mother Tongue, Ewe. By choice, I have so far held back from publishing my Ewe language poetry in print. Instead, I have settled for publishing them as audio recordings. Both *Agbenɔxevi* and *GhanaNya* were released as cassette and cd recordings as far back as 2001. The immediate impact of these audio-recorded Ewe poems on countless listeners was an important revelation for me. Following the introduction of some of the *Agbenɔxevi* and *GhanaNya* poems to radio listeners in Togo, thanks to the publicity given them by the late Dr. Ephrem Dorkenoo, these poems in Ewe were selected for Le grand Prix de poesie en langue nationale [Ewe], by Rencontre International Des

Createurs En Poesie [RICEP], Lome, Togo [2007]. One significant point about these poems is the fact that some of them are *recreations* (not *translations*) in Ewe of earlier versions written and published in English. Thus, *Agbenɔxevi* in Ewe is a much more elaborate version of the sequence 'Akofa', which first appeared in *A Harvest of Our Dreams*.

Lessons learned from the special appeal of these Ewe poems as recorded voice made me see a need for releasing my English language poems in *PraiseSong for TheLand* with a companion cd a year later in 2002. *The Place We Call Home* was also released with a double CD. As Kofi Awoonor observes in his Foreword:

> The value of this new volume, *PraiseSong for TheLand*, which combines print with sound, is the ultimate homage that the poet pays to the intimate and elemental force of voice, the first instrument of poetry. Song, chant, call it what you wish, is the primary vehicle of all poetry. Print is the recent stepchild. Without the magical force of the original vehicle, poetry is less sacred, less ample as the ultimate expression of human creativity (p. 11).

Beyond *PraiseSong for TheLand* and *The Place We Call Home*, here now is *SeedTime - Selected Poems I*, a backward glance to those magical years of birth waters flowing across a landscape filled at once with danger and hope, with dying and rebirth in the mystery and miracle of new beginnings so soon after countless brushfires. But the doubt returns again so close behind the hope as we offer trembling prayers in *new poems from an old loom: See What They've Done To Our Sunrise*. Yet, somehow, we must open our minds and souls to the Forever Promise of New SeedTimes. This world cannot, must not crumble under our watch.

West Legon, Accra. August 8, 2019.

Selections from **AncestralLogic & CaribbeanBlues**

The Taino in 1992

for Manuel Vargas   for Wilson Harris

Ao! Amigo   Los Amigos

Adios   Domingo
Adios   Santo Domingo

Hispaniola   Hispaniola   Hispaniola
Lost Land of the Taino

Christoph Colomb   Christoph Colomb
Duarte   Sanchez   Mella
Imperial Statues in a Sea of Blood.

The Turbulent Memory of the Taino
And a Hurricane of Arawak Sounds.

So they wiped them out
Drowned their screams
Burned their nerves and bones
And scattered their ashes
Across the intimidating splendour
Of this young history of lies.

StormTime in these CaribSeas.

Soon the Hurricanes   the Hurricanes
Shall Spring Loose
From places of Ancient Ambush.

They will gather once more
The Ancestral Anger
Of this Land of Hostile Winds.

In the Dying Howl
Of Hurricane Columbus
We yet may hear once more
The Rising Growl
Of the Taino Chieftain
Who opted out of Christ's Kingdom
Where they insist the Butcher Dog
May come to sup with ArchAngel and God.

Through infinities of Centuries
Forever lost to Trauma and to Amnesia

We ford Ancient Oceans of Blood
In that Final Backward Glance

Into Old Chambers
Jammed with Precious Stones

And first fruits gathered in Savage
Haste from fields nurtured with Love
By those Careful Guardians of the Earth:

> "We do not inherit the Earth
> from our Ancestors
> We borrow it from our Children."

Christoph Colomb   Christoph Colomb
Hispaniola   Hispaniola   Hispaniola

Adios   Domingo
Adios   Santo Domingo

San Pedro De Macoris
for Marino

In these CaneFields
Nourished by Silent
Groans of Haitian Immigrants

The Memory Caves
in upon History's Sad Logic:

Disinherited by Haiti
Repudiated by Republica Dominicana
They Shuffle through Life
In the uncertain Dance of the Zombi.

These are the Children
of Macandal and Toussaint
of Dessaline and Olivoro Mateo.

But ancestral trophies
Are no valid collateral
For the new industrial enterprise.

Across infinite sadness
of plantations of
sorrow now grown to harvest point

We intrude upon Secrets
As Ancient and Modern
As Inconsolable Hurts
In Armpits of our Joys.

On the Batey you must explain
Abel Williams:
Head of Household at 18.
Has never known a Girl.
May never know Woman.
And he is Head of a Family of 8.
Proud Inheritor of a Father
Who Poured out his Life
Upon the SugarFields.

And I search for answers Still.

And Dear Marino   do Not
Wonder Why I could Not
Drink the Coffee you Made
With so much Love and Care
As we paused for breath in your Home:

I could Not Take
The Café-au-Lait.
I could Not take it Black.
But above all
I could Not take BitterSugar.

The Haitian Batey
Is a LivingWound
In the Throat of the SugarMill.

RenewalTime

Into the Nerve Centre
Of these Memory Fields

A Taino Ancestor Bursts
Plants his Hopes into Towers
Above retreating Usurper Gods.

Tall.   Proud.
Naked. Erect

Like a Divine Phallus
Ready to Explode
Countless ManSeeds
Into WomanEarth for the Coming FertileTime.

HavanaSoul

For Amando Entralgo
For Claritta Pullido

So I made the ultimate connection
Between two lifetimes set apart
By a final death of old mythologies.

And on Havana Bay
Along the Malecon
Down the Marina Hemingway

I stand breathless with yearning for strange desires
As the fading sun
Sets my memory ablaze with sparks and fireflies.

At the Marina Hemingway   I stood among
Strange shadows of the imagination and heard
Once more the distant call of the inner life of things.
Old Ernest in his greatness looked upon
The calm before the hurricanes and planted
His OldMan's Dreams where the Ocean Perch
And the Blue Shark may never come to feed.

And Santiago de Cuba Haunts me into Dawn and Dream:

Daisy Castilo   the far away look in her eyes
Speaking soft and deep of how her mother
Welcomed Marcus Garvey
to Havana of the Stormy Years
Her mother - still alive with a mind as sharp as a laser beam -
Had seen this little finger of Earth stick out in troubled years.
Seen her Cuba's run for life survive Baptista's birth & death
Had seen her Island Solitude rise to new glory
in the east-west trail Antonio Maceo
once carved along the mountain slopes.

And this indeed is Cuba of the fabled Bay of Pigs?

The Royal Palm
Standing still among her Island Solitude:

Tall.   Proud.   Erect
against the Storm.
Full of Erotic Energy.
And yet overwhelmed
By ecstasy of victories
Won in a Sea of Hurricanes

LYING LOW & DEEP IN ARMPIT OF THE BUFFALO
BULL.

Now that you've lost all friends
To Freedom Cyclones of our time
For how long may you survive
The inspiring hate of enemies?
For how long must all your goals
Be measured between angles
set by devoted opponents?

Suppose the inevitable logic of history
Rolls in upon the hurricane
deprives you of your dearest enemy
would you still be firm and steady and royal like the palm?
Or will you loosen your hold on the prime purpose for which
Jose Marti   Antonio Maceo   Che Guevara
And the endless line of valiant ancestors
Fought their own doubts and died their own deaths
So that life may be deprived of its eternal hesitations?

I go back now to Baby Joys I left
back home in tender care
of Little Folk with Giant Dreams
who bet their children's last hope
against the boasts of Tyrant Kings.

No one flies the Middle Passage now
and for lack of friends along the way
CubanaAir must take me first
to Gander of the Intemperate North
Then south to Madrid of the Arid Lands.
And AirFrance into Paris.
And SwissAir into Zurich.
and on and on
To GoldCoast via IvoryCoast
Those sometime Treasure Lands
where now we must embrace the Orphan Life
in small measures of Foreign Aid.

And all our journeys must always take us
Away from Destinations into disLocations
Until one day   tired at last from Endless
Trailings of Lost Purpose and Lost Vision
We mark the only Straight Route
from Ghana to Havana to Guyana
And on and on to Savanna
in Georgia of the Deep Deep South.

With AfricanaAirways
we re-navigate the Middle Passage
clear the old debris and Freshen the Waters
with Iodine and Soul-Chlorine

AND our Journey into SoulTime
Shall be
The Distance between the Eye and the Ear.

Lolita Jones[1]

for Dzifa   for Maya

And so they says ma Name is Lolita Jones?

But that aint ma real Name
I never has known ma Name our Name

I cud'a been Naita   Norwetu
Or may be Maimouna   Mkabayi
Asantewaa   may be Aminata   Malaika.

Ma Name cud'a been Sculptured
Into colors of the Rainbow
Across the bosom of our Earth.

But you see:
Long ago   your People sold ma People.
Ma People sold to Atlantic's Storms.

The Storms   first it took away our Voice
Then it took away our Name
And it tried to strip us of our Soul.

---

1 The occasion is that of the death in exile of Kwame Nkrumah, the deposed First President of Ghana. There is an imaginary trial going on in Ghana to decide whether he deserves to be brought back home for a hero's burial. Lolita Jones is the final and uninvited witness, testifying to Nkrumah's Pan African legacy. See "In the High Court of Cosmic Justice", in my earlier collection *Earthchild* (Accra: Woeli Publishing Services, 1985).

Since then   we've been Pulled   Pushed
Kicked   Tossed   Squeezed   Pinched
Knocked Over   Stepped Upon   and Spat Upon.

We've been All Over the Place
And yet
We Ain't Got Nowhere At All.

That's why when the Black Star Rose
I flew over to find ma Space

And aint nobody like this Brother
Who gave me back ma Soul.

But you   you Kicked him out
                you Pushed him off
                you Segregated him from his SoilSoul.

And yet since that Fucking Day
You all aint done Nothing worth a Dime!

Now his Soul is Gone on Home
You sit out here   you Mess your Head
You drink palm wine   you Talk some Shit
Just Shuckin' n Jivin' n Soundin'
All Signifyin' Nothin'!
You all just Arguin' Funerals.

Aint nothing gone down here at all
And you all is nothing worth ma pain.

I'll gather ma tears around ma wounds
I'll fly me off to ma QueenDom Come.

I've got me a date with our SoulBrother
And this aint no place for our Carnival.

Just hang out here
       And grind your teeth
       And cry some mess
       And talk some bull
       And drive some corpse to his KingDom Gone.

Why dont you talk of Life for a change?
You all is so hung up with the Dead
And I aint got no time to die just now.

I cudnt care to wait for the judgment of your Gods.
There never was no case against our SoulBrother.

It's you all is on trial here
But I cudnt care to wait
And hang you even by the Toe.

       You didnt even invite me here at all.
       But I came   &   I Spoke ma Soul

Nostalgia

Above all   I shall forever
lament the wisdom
of those many many

Friends who disinherited their Souls
And chose the Misery of Alien Joys.

    trapped in circles among SnowFields
    their Spirits Freeze   and Thaw   and Frost
    with Constant Fickleness of NorthernWinds.

Once   too often
they Converge in Smokey PartyRooms
Drinking Hard   to Prove
a Point only they   can see   can feel
Arguing Endless Justifications
for a Choice Sadly Made.

Between their Dreams of Fame
Their Hopes of Instant Wealth

the Nostalgic Self Moans its Way
through MidNight Storms
into DawnNightmares

    Reaching into   Distances   Silences...

Memories Alone are not enough SoulGuide
Into Futures Flled with many Absences.

Children of the Land[2]

A Sequence for African Liberation

i:

WE are the Children of the Northern Lands.

Our hopes have known the fury of sands and storms.
But like the rolling Saharas of our history
Our dreams have flourished among the oases.

From the mountain peak of Toubkal of the Atlas
We shout our joys across the space of sands

   all the way to Tahat in Ahaggar
   all the way to Tousside in Tibesti

From the Atlantic Coast to the Red Sea
From the ancient Straight of Gibraltar

   along the seaboard of the Mediterranean
   all the way to Alexandria of our Past and our Future

---

2 Originally composed at the request of the Ghana National Commission on Children, for a Flag-Raising Ceremony at the O.A.U. Monument, Accra. The performance involved selected children from some schools in Accra, July 1984. See a discussion of the dramatization of this first version of the poem in my essay "Poetry as Dramatic Performance: The Ghana Experience." *Research in African Literatures* 22.2 (Summer 1991).

From the Northern Lands
We come to you with all the wishes of our People.

WE are the Children of the Northern Lands.

ii.

WE are the Children of the Eastern Lands.
    the lands of the Rising Sun.

Once so long   our hopes were ambushed
    by the Children of the Panther.
But by the fighting skills of our warriors
    we broke the Panther 's jaw and pride.

Today   we fold our dreams gently in our arms.

Like the Rift Valleys of our ancient lands
Our roots cut deep into the bosom of our Earth.

With the splendour of Zebra and of Gazelle
With the miracle and the majesty of the Giraffe
We measure our height against the ancient pride
Of mountains: the Karisimbi the Ruwenzori the Kilimanjaro.

Our land's beauty is larger than the dream of praise singers.

Our hopes rise deep from the bosom of our Earth
And touch the very forehead of the Sky.

From the mountain glories of our Eastern Lands
We come to you with the victories the worries of our People:

WE are the Children of the Eastern Lands.

iii.

WE are the Children of the Western Lands.
    the lands of the Falling Sun.

Once so long   the Children of the Polar Bear
    set upon our Dream and Tore it into Shreds.

But by the cunning of our Warriors of our Elders
    by the Divine intervention of the Mosquito
Today our hopes rise higher than the Eagle's Pride.

We who once did all the farming and the cooking
We'll watch Bear Children feast themselves to Death.

Today we know the taste of Freedom's many Joys and Pains.

From the Fouta Djalon to the Adamawa
We spread our hopes into the Colours of the Rainbow.

Along the Gambia   and the Volta   and the Niger
We channel our anger into the living waters of our harvest Joys.

We've known many seasons before the Killer Drought:
the abundance of ancient Ghana and of Mali and of Songhai.
In our future   we dream again the rising Harvest Moon.

From ancient mysteries of the Western Lands
We greet you today with the secret wisdom of our People:

WE are the Children of the Western Lands.

iv.

WE are the Children of the Central Lands

We who once Wept in the Valleys
    of the Kasai and the Sangha
Today   our Hopes Rise Higher
      than Flood Waters of the Kongo.

There once were those who thought
    we would die the shameful death of lepers.
Today   we carry our life
    in the bright flames of our eyes.

Our Hopes have Stumbled
    down the great boulders of Stanley Falls
But still   we flow on through to Lualaba
    and to our various lakes of Rest of Peace.

The Children of the Earth
must live to taste the many Joys of Earth.

WE are the Children of the Central Lands.

v:

WE are the Children of the Southern Lands.

We have seen much better times of our Earth.
Once more in Time
we shall inherit the Peace of our Earth.
We who now Moan in the Night of Gold Diggers.

Where was it heard before
    that Shaka's Children Burn in Flames
    and Die in Holes dug into his Earth?
But that's how it's been with us.

By the Miracle of our own Minds and Hands
We shall Carve away the Tiger's Claws.

We did it once to the Panther and the Lion and the Bear.
We'll do it and do it once more to the Tiger and his Greed.

From Cabinda round the Cape of Storms
and up to Cape Delgado
We'll once more Sleep and Dream and Work in Peace.

Those who now taste the Honey of Freedom's Bread
They've known also the Blood of Death
    we down South still Carry in our Voice.

Namibia shall be FREE!!   *Azania shall be FREE!!!*

From the Southern Lands of Life-Through-Death

We bring to you our people's Fears and Hopes:

WE are the Children of the Southern Lands
and
WE ALL are the Children of AFRICA!!!

Air Zimbabwe: En Route Victoria Falls

for Chris Hesse   for Samora Machel

ZamBia   ZamBezi   ZimBabwe

ZimBabwe   ZamBezi   ZimZambia

History is but the Future

We should have known in the Past

    So one of these days

    Old Victoria shall have

    to Gather her Wayward Children Home.

    If Only she knew. If Only.

ZimBabwe   ZamBezi   ZimZambia

    The mysteries of these lands

    Are deeper   loftier than

    The EmpireBuilder's dreams

    And so Victoria flows

    In Majestic Pride

    To the yawning edge of Time:

    And Great Victoria

    Falls   Tumbling

    Down the LivingStones more ancient

    Than our vision's fartherest point

    More slippery than our sleekest mossy glide.

Mutare   Rusape   Harare
Chirendzi   Chipinge   Chirundu
Chimanimani   Bulawayo   Mbalabala

The Souls of these Names
Are older than the Time
We count across our Mind's Spaces.

Mosi oua Tunya!   *Mosi oua Tunya!*

They are **The Smoke That Thunders!**
Gathering whispers of centuries
Into storms and CannonBlasts!
Mowing Great ZimBabwe down to countless ruins
Bringing silence to The Monomotapa's praise.

If Only they knew.   If Only.

If Only David knew of how
Those Stones outlived
The Monomatapa's Dreams.
If Only Cecil knew of how
Those Canyon Roads slashed Deep Wounds
Across our Earth's Belly.

If Only they knew.   If Only.

History is but the Future
We should have known in the Past.

So one of these days
Poor Victoria shall have
To trek her dream across her own safari of pain
Poor Victoria shall have
To go back home to her QueenDom Gone.

If only she knew.   If Only.

ZimBabwe   ZamBezi   ZimZambia.

If Only.   If Only She Knew.

Victoria-

FALLS....................!

HarareBlues

to Herbert Chimhundu
&
for The Liberators in Search of Liberation

At the end of the BloodTrail
In aftermath of VictorySongs

we young veterans of armed combat
are left abandoned & stranded
on the outskirts of the new life:

Once   we Dropped
            Out of School   Out of Trade   Out of Life.
We took up guns
            to reclaim the lost ancestral land.
            to re-name and re-own the land.

With Blood Flowing Freely From our Souls
We dammed the tide against the Storms.

In deep forests   in desperate caves   and grave trenches
Death roared around our heads our lives our souls

            snatched from our arms lifelong comrades
            tore them apart & threw them back
            at us: Dismembered Beyond Reclaim.

But there was a hope that always kept
Our spirits floating above the carnage

The land we knew and loved with such fearsome hope
Covered our footprints with gentle stirrings of the soil.

And then one day at noon   they Set our Night Ablaze
with Bonfires.   Suspended Battle Cries.   Composed
An Anthem Tattooed with Hopes & Lingering Doubts.

One day at noon   Peacemakers Came
and Set our Night Ablaze with Bonfires.
Abolished our Battle Songs   and Planted
their Mulatto Constitution in our Soul.

Then they marched us back to LowFields
and
To Old TownShips still Stranded in the Storm.

And the pastured land Flows Like Troubled Dreams
into Endless Mirages along the Distant Rainbow Line.

And we who once roamed the deep forests
And shared our land's secret seeds with bird & beast
Are now hurdled into little corners of the nation's life
so utterly stranded among the rotten stench
Of Harare's secret wounds & hidden traps.

In our eyes Old Flames of Hope now Smoulder
into Volcanic Embers   Burning Silent Streams
of Venomous Gas Leakage into the City's Ventricles.

With arms forever outstretched into solitude
We drink down our permanent anger
From spectacular calabashes so large
They must contain the overspill of war memories.

Beware   Brother   Beware
Beware the hand that reaches down:

Each tattered bosom hides a knife more
Deadly than the Venomous Viper's Fangs.

Each night   in a Flash of Steel
The blood still flows into old sewers
Irrigating the soil and draining down
Sacrificial lives in hope to appease

The Souls that Won the War   But Lost the Peace.

DesertStorm

for Naana & for Obiba

..... So I Flew into Old London
in that Night of the Death-Line
for Saddam &
for his Warrior Angels of the Apocalypse.

The Heavens broke loose next day,
you remember?
and all we do now
is listen   even in our sleep
to the screaming hysteria
of war tales told in relentless relay
of Uncle Sam's Braggart Boys.

It is the Age of Old Generals
all dressed in Shiny Medals
issuing Hourly Briefs
from Cozy Conference Rooms.
And out there in the Gulf
A Widowed Mother's Only Son
Bleeds to Death in DesertStorms.

And all the President's Men
say it is the Greatest Thing to Do:

To Call for War and Watch the War
from the Safe Distance
of a WhiteHouse Fortified
Against the Raging Tide of Blood
Against the Lurking Danger of the ArmedBush.

And after Glorious Booms
of the StarWars Show
the Ruthless Logic of War
takes over and Drives us All--
Inevitably   they say--
Back into Sad Old Times
where War is Not   CanNot be
a Game of Kids Played on VideoScreens
by InfantMen   but a Meal of Death
Cooked in Blood and Served RedHot
at FlashPoint of Gun&Smoke
and the Choked Breath.

And when it is all over
we shall once more Inherit
a Generation of Cracked Souls
for whom we must Erect New
Monuments and Compose New
Anthems of Praise and the Eternal Hope of Life
Beyond the Recurring Stupidity of War Heroes.

January 31, 1991.

Santrofi

for Jack Mapanje

I.
Santrofi   Santrofi   Santrofi

against persistent rumours
of your midnight
death by stabbing squads
I must compose this suicide note
in stupid solidarity with a foolish friend.

Like you   my mind is burdened
with ancestral indiscretion.
The slightest lie
gives us indigestion
so we must go gathering dangerous rumours
letting our minds loose on laxative
soiling popular images of decent people.

They say it is sad for a full-grown
Man with children who call him
Papa   to stagger home in tears.

But Santrofi   I couldnt help maself.

When I heard they say they say
they picked you up at deaf of night

I could not hold on to my pride.

I broke up in fears   I crumbled
home sobbing through my tears.

II.

But then the children started wailing.

So I laughed.   I laughed I told them
I was rehearsing my part in a difficult play.

So they laughed.   The children laughed.
But then they asked to see my script
so they could cheer and prompt me on.

Santrofi   I had to explain
there was no script to our play.

We act it out by daily dress rehearsals
of the various things we shouldn't do.

The drama unfolds backward
with every step we take forward.

The plot quickens and complicates
with unexpected & twisted
re-enactments of scenes from future dreams.

We are hurled into false resolutions
leaving us still entangled in strange
sub-plots
forever groping for redirection
back into our main
conflict with its knotted
quest for a breath of air
free of all toxic substances.

We grow breathless yearning
for escape from suffocating assemblies
of shameless men with their poisonous speech
persuading us all to die once more
and die all over again.

But Santrofi   against
their kind offer
of death by stabbing squads
we must insist on our dream
of life   our dream
of life   our dream
of life among the burning grass
    life among the riding storms
       among the desert sands
of life among the thunderbolts.

III.

Santrofi   Santrofi   Santrofi

you remember how
often I came for you at dawn
our shotguns loaded and ready
for the ancestral partridge hunt?

We were such great bad shots
Our bullets ran away from our game.

But we always came back home.
We always came back home.
Back home to our meal of modest
corn and fish and life.
We always came back home.

So when your Maimouna
in a voice grown eerie with sudden pain
told of how
some nervous men with tangled beards
came for you & walked you
into the deepness of their night
 fiercely clutching stolen rifles

I have been wondering
what BigGame Hunters Club
you may have joined on secret oath.

I have listened every night and every dawn
for the lonely echo of the hunter's call

But all I hear is this silence
deeper than the liar's yawn.

IV.

Santrofi   Santrofi   Santrofi

so now   I am guilty.   Guilty
of harbouring doubts and fears

doubts for their smiles
fears for your mind
fears for your life
fears fears fears for those joys
we dared to dream for our land.

I suppose they'll come with pincers
probing our tongue for unspoken curses.

And we wish we could hold our breath forever.

But once too often we've held
our doubts and found unspeakable
terror in silence and patience
when marvelous blockheads
took up megaphones and broke
eardrums with philosophical obscenities

and baboons in mufti & native sandals
made menacing speeches from platforms

borne on shoulders of those who chose

patience and silence in spite of doubts
silence and patience in spite of doubts

in spite of bleeding fear
in spite of leaking hurt

silence and patience in spite of doubts
patience and silence in spite of doubts.

Santrofi   Santrofi   Santrofi.

V.

Santrofi   Santrofi   Santrofi

you remember
how once upon our doubts
they planted letters in the press

and in the guise of mythical voices
they painted our names with dung and slime?

Santrofi   Santrofi   Santrofi

VI.

Santrofi   Santrofi   Santrofi

Today   the fierce young ones
who broke the dawn with smoking guns
are now become Youthful Elders of State.

How come
    they see so much guilt
    in every elder's eyes?
    and hear so much betrayal
    in every intellectual's sneeze?

They bypassed warnings
and took huge loans
only to import
halfwits from
harvard & princeton
halfwits & gifted inventors
of designer deaths
in man-made seasons of drought.

Santrofi   Santrofi   Santrofi

you must lay ambush at Hell Gate
and watch them trespass into Limbo
and lead them stranded and Lost
among the Ghosts of False Prophets.

and do us a favour   will you?
Throw a little red pepper in their eyes.
And do Not Wipe Away their Tears.

Angels may come and offer you QueenDoms
But whatever you do
Do Not Wipe Away their Tears.   Eh! Santrofi!!

Bayonets

BEFORE the Season of the Bayonet
    there was the Season of the Hoe
    a Season of the Soul's Harvest:

    We Grew Wonder-eyed Standing
    Humbled before the Miracle
    of the Giant Oak Locked Deep
    Down within the Tiniest Mystery Seed.

    In those Seasons of our Soul's Harvest
    there were Such Fires in our Eyes.
    Our Spirits Flowered and Petalled
    into Hues of Faintest Rainbows
    offering New and Newer Images
    of Dreams we could with Ten Fingers
    Mould into Things and Thoughts and Hopes.

THEN   they came with BullDozers.
And Then   the ArmouredCars   Dressed in Camouflage.

    NOW   we Plant Grenades in Backyard Farms
    Harvesting Coffins
    in Showers of Bullets and FirePower.

    They Pick our Flesh on Bayonets.

    Across Cold Muzzles of Guns
    They Break our Sleep in Two
    Give one half to CannonBlast
    Toss one half into Silence Deeper
    Than Volcano's Bleeding Core.

There will be Showers at SunRise
And Storms at SunDrown.
Bones shall Sprout Tendrils more Verdant
Than the Loveliest GreenMamba.

Rivulets of Venom shall Water our Fields
Restoring this Soil to Ancestral Fertile Time.

Guilt

i.
And they opened up his wound.
Polished its tender surface
With alligator pepper
And onion paste.

But his soul was large
Enough to hold his hurt.

Grasping Tight
To sharp painpoint of Breath
He threw them back that Final
Look
Whose depths they feared to explore.

A Look Suspended
Somewhere
Between surprise and wonder
Carefully balanced
Between desire to
Hope
And the need to
Believe
That Fear   sometimes
Is a noble retreat from
Doom.

ii.
He swore he would be Human   If
Only they would let him   Be.

But they Hanged Him all the Same.

Except that even in Death
They could not Look him in the Face.

There were such Questions
On lips of this Corpse
Whose memory survives Life   survives Death.

The LawMakers don themselves
in weeds thick enough
To parry the thorniest Question Mark.

The HangMen gather
Their Courage around their Fear
Assuring themselves in whispers
Even they themselves cant hear:

   It really was a Duty by The Law.

But they Hanged Him all the Same.
And they couldn't Look him in the Face.

Redeemers

They came with a Bouquet of CobWebs
Sang obscene songs
Over our sacred images
Their huge nostrils still clogged
With dust and steamy breath.

They were sent to persuade us all
Against our very selves
So we in our delusion
Would deny our own follies
Spending seasons pretending to Divinity.

But our Human flesh stuck to our bones
Like sweat on dirt on goosepimples
Stuck to our bones like dirt on sweat
Till our Souls stood naked and humbled
Before noble passions that moved us still
Even among our many blunders.

We stood among our many broken dreams.
And oh we saw our old follies kneel in low profile
Against the blazing Western Sky.

They came with a Bouquet of Cobwebs
Sang obscene songs
Over our sacred images of Self and Gods
Their huge nostrils still clogged
With dust and steamy breath.
In their hands a kind offer of Holy Death.

But our Human flesh stuck to our bones
And noble passions still move us on
Even among our many blunders.

History & Blindness

Once we snatched our heads
from jaws of Polar Bear

And now with our own hands
we offer our hearts for safe-keeping
to the Panther Prowling Round
the Outskirts of our Lives
reclining under ancestral communal trees
laying ambush in that midday snooze
in which even dreams
take on the density of fear.

Let us not deceive ourselves
believing the future is
but a photocopy of the past.

If the wisdom of the elders
were proof against disasters

their hopes would not have lost
heirlooms in the noonday
spark that set the sea ablaze.

Old Lizard

I am Old Lizard
with my Stomach Aches
Stuck Away
under the Rhythm of my Breath.

I Laugh Rainbows
through screams into many miles of hurt
through pains that stretch into endless memory.

Only the Setting Sun
Can tell what treasures lay
Beyond the mountain clouds.
But Children of Butterfly
now wrap themselves
in Borrowed Velvet Robes
Hop the skies and Dare the Rays
Pretending
They are Chosen Inheritors
Of our Sun's Glory.

And I who scaled the Loftiest Dizzy Heights
Fallen off the Tallest Odum Tree
I've peeped over Horizon's Final Curtained Stop.
And
I've seen our Sun Retreat
Before the Blanket Anger of the Night.

So I can only nod and nod and nod my Head
In knowing Futility of Velvet's Dreams.

Let ButterFly Children hope and dream the skies
in Borrowed Velvet Robes
Pretending
they are Chosen Inheritors
of our Sun's Glory.

I can only nod and nod and nod my Burdened Head
I   Old Lizard   with my Stomach Aches
Stuck Away under the Rhythm of my Breath.

Novimɔ

RainDrop in the Sun.

She was a Rain-
Drop in our Sun.

In her Gentle
Breeze of Voice
She Caught all
Splendours of our World.

And in her Deep
Ripples of Breath
Our Rivers Found
Primordial Confluence with Stars.

HusagoDance

One day   quite simply
I shall set one brief
Step upon the long
Road into SoulSpace.

With a teasing grin
On my stupid face
I shall take a final
Look at all the things
I should have done.

Somewhere Up on a tiny
Branch of our ancestral tree
I shall perch and watch
The *Husago* Drums
Dance Life out of Death.

A Love Supreme

Beyond Beauty of the Body
There is Beauty of the Mind.

Beyond Beauty of the Mind.
There is Beauty of the Person.

Beyond Beauty of the Person.
There is Beauty of the Soul.

From RestLess Joys of FretFul Love
I Trace Glories into the Contours of Your Mould.

I Trace the Topo-Beauty of Your Soul
In the Gentle Rise & Fall & Curve of Lips & Hips.

My Passions Rise & Fall & Break
Like Surfs upon Your Many Shores.

Along Your Spinal Stretch of Rift Valleys
I Stumble Into
Deep & Secret Joys of Love & Peace.

In QuickSands of Ancient MysteryCaves
I Feel Eternity Flash across Horizons of My Mind
Then   The Bottom Drops Out of My Breath!

Selections from EARTHCHILD

Akasanoma Hadzixevi

for Akua

My Fears become Visions
my Visions Give birth to Words
my words become the Toddler's Joy
Stumbling through our Village Lanes our Sandy Shores

I make Words Give Birth to BushFires
my Skies go Wild with Glow-Words and FireFlies
Still our Children Die of *Kwashiorkoric* Pains
So I Abandon Words to Harvest Dreams of MythMakers
Spending Seasons Digging Up our Old FarmLands
now Grown Full of Serpent Egg and Thorn
We Burn the Thorn to Memory and to Ash
Teach the Soil the Fertile Time of Infant Corn
And Stalks of Maize now Stand so Tall so Proud
All with Growing Babies on their Back

Then Comes a Storm from Setting Place of Sun
Blows WhirlWinds across my Children's Children's
Dreams.   And they Drive me Back to Words
to ButterFlies and FireFlies and MythMaking

I am become the Singer Bird with Ecstasies of Pain
I Gather Dawns and Pluck Feathers from RainBow Gods

I Take from Earth her Gift of Songs
I Give the World our Choice of Words our Infant Corn

Akasanoma . . . Akasanoma . . . Akasanoma . . .
Hadzixevi . . . Hadzixevi . . . Hadzixevi . . .
Agbenɔxevi . . . Agbenɔxevi . . . Agbenɔxevi . . .

Take my Children's Children's Dreams
Give them Back to Time to Space and All Time
Fly them through Eternity to Eternity
Sort them out with Infinite Care with Old Wisdom
Tie them all into Lost Cycles to Future Lives
Float them Far Far Away. Above Beyond the Reach of Storms.

HoneyComb for BeeChildren

For Every Dirge Adidi Sang
I now Must Weave a Song of New Birth-Cords
I Must Put a Hand on the Funeral Drums
Send Away the Chief Mourners
Break Death's Pot at Kutonu
Watch Crab Children Crawl Away to Mermaid's Call

I could Blow WhirlWinds
and Ride the Storm to Kutsiami
Bring Him Home to Festivals of Peace

Long before the Reign of ThunderClouds
we were RainBow's Favoured Child
we Wore our Gown of Velvet Flames
we Took Long Walks on Sky SideWalks
Arm-in-Arm with Xebieso

The Twilight Zone our Meeting Place with Stars
our Breath a Gentle Stirring of the Soul
We Spoke with Voice of Cuckoo Birds
We Drank MoonBeams from Lips of SunFlowers

BeeChildren with Ecstasies in our Eyes
we Dance Fortune in Cross-Rhythms
we Hum our Joy to Mother-Queen at Dawn
Build our Hopes in Arms of Guardian Baobab Trees
Turn our Back to ThunderClaps
to Lightning's Brief Skirmish

We Swarm Around our HoneyComb
We Watch ReBirth of BeeQueendom.

Austin: May 21, 1982

In the Corners of Her Eyes

for Janis

There was a Rainbow in the Corners of her Eyes
        Giving Birth to Butterfly and Song
        Whispering Through the Corneas of the Soul
        Waking Up the Memories Lost to Time
But they Brought Neon-Lights at Twilight Hour
They Robbed the Soul of all Vision

Those Many Hues of Fantasy Hour
        were Streaks of Joy from Lost Planets
They were Last Flickers of Broken Stars

So she used to Stand Tip-Toe on Old Corners of Life
Cooing a Love Song for her Sunrise Twilight Dreams:

        Who Then shall Gather our MoonBeams in their Eyes
        And Carry our DayDreams in their Souls
        And Polish our Voice Box with their Songs
        And Spread our Moon Dust All Over their Brows?

        The Sun may Walk Away from us at Dawn
        His Old Splendour Subdued by Lightning's Brief Anger

        Say   Who Then shall Gather our Laughters into
        Sound Dunes that Roll Skywards to Vision's End?

But her Lover Came Back Home from the Wars
Long After they Put his Name Among
the Young Warriors who Fell on Alien Fields
to Raise the Names of Alien Kings and Alien Queens
She Met him at the Cemetery Gates
Still Holding Out her Laughter on his Palms
They Stopped to Check the Memorial Stone
They Scraped his Name to Powdery Fine Nothing
They Gave it Back to Earth. Then
They Walked Away Toward the Rising Place of Suns.

　　　　and Now   we Know there Never Shall Be
　　　　any Memorials for Our Race
　　　　Except Of Course These Laughters in Our Soul

Rodney[3]

Another Time   Another Bomb   Some Other Soul

We do Not Know the Faces of God
We do not Care for Moses and his Dreams

Have we Not Known the Dreams of Infant Corn?
         the Hopes of ButterFlies?
         the Joys of TurtleDoves?
Have we Not been the Rosebud in the Fields?
         the Honey-Suckling Bee?
         the Dimpled Dreams of Young Maidens?
Have we not Borne the RainBow in Our Eyes?

There are Memories in our Garbage Cans
Full of Bits of History's Junk
and Those who Claim they Own the Earth
have Now become Devotees of Death
Scavenging our BackYards
for Tattered Bits of Hopes we Put Away
in Small Corners in Broken Cooking Pots

---

3   Dr Walter Rodney, noted Pan-Africanist historian and political
activist, died in June 1980 when a walkie-talkie devise given him by
a "friend" exploded in his brother's car in the streets of Georgetown,
Guyana.

Today the Burning Rods of Old Burnham
came at Dawn and Took Walter Away
They say it was a Walkie-Talkie Trick
the Cruel Joke of God's Children
And the Old Man in his Old Wisdom
still Waits for Judgement Day

We do Not Know the Faces of God
We Cannot Care for Moses and his Dreams
In these Hours of the Mourning
our Souls have Sat on Stone Benches
Counting Time in HeartBeats of the Storm

Where were the Children of Tenge Dzokoto
when MoonMen Came at MidNight Hour?
Our Hunters Swear they Saw the MidNight Dance
            the Feast on Flesh
            the Feast on Warm Entrails

They Swear they Heard the Screams of Infant Souls
Where Then were the Children of Thunder
while Moon Men Rode the MidNight Storm
Vomiting Scorn Upon Our Infant Joys?

We have not been the Tools of Fools
although the Finer Urges of our Being
have Grown so Blunt from Careless Hands
       of Small-Faced Men

They Swear they Own the Earth on which we Shit
and there are no Disposable Diapers
for the Droppings of the Poor
so they Lick our arse with Tongues of Flame
But come Fertility Time and History's Garbage Dumps
shall give New Birth to the Hunter's Dog
to Hunt the Hunter Down   Give him Up
to the Mystery of the Storm

And Walter shall have Found Other Groundings With His Folk
He shall have Made his Stop-Over at Heaven's Other Gate
He shall have Left his Brief Query for Grand Father:

       Dear God
       There are Bombs and Flames on Earth
       that Put HellFire to Shame
       And MoonChildren in Their Greed
       Have Eaten Up Our Earth

Memory's Call

for Neto and Biko

I

But Who are Those with Teeth of Stolen Gold
Selling Smiles to GrandChildren of SunGoddess?
Let them Ask their GodFathers
for Remembrances of their Ancestral Feasts of Blood

Forgive my Song my God.   Perhaps   sometimes
my Voice shall Knock on Those Abandoned Doors
the Finger Nails of Thought Shall Pluck the Glaze
        from Memory's Eyes

        I Hear the Harvest Songs of MoonChildren
        But Where are All the Planters Gone?

There Once were Men in All these fields
Making Love to Fertile Soils: the Caress
the Stirring Rhythmic Beat   the Frenzied
Screams of Machete Blades Slashing Through
the Warm Embrace of Earth
And Now   the WindFall Harvest Dance

        I Hear the Harvest Gatherers Come and Go
        But Where have All the Planters Gone?

II

So we Walked a Thousand Nights and Dawns
across SunRise into NoonTime of Our Birth

Diviners Cast their Chains across the Bosom
        of Our Song
but their Knowledge of Things they would not
        give to Words
Sometimes   There was an Argument
        a Certain Urgent Call
and the Lonely Voice Gathered Echoes
        from Skies of BattleFields

Please   Go Tell Awuno-Boko for me   that
This Panther Died in his Sleep.   But Not without a Leap.
Let no Merchants of Sorrow Come
        with Barrels on their Head
Seeking to Gather our Moans to those Distilleries of Pain
The Netos The Bikos Took Away our Funeral Songs
into House of Storms   Sending Back
the Rhythmic Throb of Infant Hopes

There are Anthems Leaping Through the Skies
and Panther's Kids are Sharpening Paws
for New HandShakes with GrandChildren
        of MoonGoddess

It is Rush-Hour in Soul-City
And on Shores of Eternity
Ghosts are Doing a Ceremonial Dance
At ReBirth of New Heroes.

III

Oh   do Not Soil the Splendour of our Duckling
although One Day She too shall Cover Herself with Mud
        and Shit Upon our Velvet Dream

Can you Not See the RainBow in Her Eyes?

There Always shall be the Slender Voice of Dreams
Harvesting Memories from RainBow's Flowered Shores
Beyond our SunBird's Festive Dance
a Harvest of Images Lie in Wait
for Memory's Call at TwiLight Time

These Muddied Fields have Known
        the Gleam of SpringWaters
But our History Broke the Laws of Space and Time
We Flowed Upwards Against the Rise of Mountain Slopes
Volcanoes Spat their Dirt Upon our Vision's Gleam

Our Children Come Crawling Through the Agonies of Birth
Holding Petals in their Farewell Call to Death
They Shall Grow in the Abundance of the Grain
their Seasons Filled with Many Harvest Joys

So Leave them Alone to Flutter their Wings
and Gather Ripples from Muddied Streams
Sowing Seeds of Joy along the Banks of Storms.

They Say Some Day these Storms Shall Burst
Into Showers of Pollen on Memory's TwiLight Zone
And our Memories are the Soul's RainClouds
Floating Through from Moments in our Past

Sometimes they Come with Storms
Sometimes they Come as Spring Showers
They Give us Back our Infant Sacred Hopes

Oh   do Not Soil the Splendour of our Duckling
Although So Soon   She Too   has Covered Herself with Mud
            and Shits Upon our Velvet Dream.

Hero and Thief

I was Counting Time in the Heartbeat of the Storm
when Fui and Enyo came Riding through WhirlWinds
She with the Dream Beauty of New RainBows and
He in his Quiet Way Spoke of How
a Nervous Government Sits on our Bankrupt Stool
Wearing a Gown of Fantasy and Hope
Telling Tales of Foreign Aid and GodMothers
          at Christmas Time. . .

Is it Enough we Search the Private Dreams of Poets
          when our Land's Nightmares Give Birth
          to Strange Desires
and our Children Draw their Wishes in QuickSands
          of this Earth?
Is it Enough   is it Enough we Probe the Pampered
          Dreams of Poets
while our People Scratch the Dunghills of this Earth
where Once the Flowers Bloomed and Poured Perfume
upon the Pestilence of Rotten Memories?
Is it Enough   is it Enough we Dream in Foreign Languages
and Drink Champagne in Banquet Halls of a Proud People
while Our People Crack Palm Kernels with their Teeth?

          It is Not enough   it Isn't Enough
          to Go in Search of The Lone Hero
          while the Common Thief Inherits our Ancient Stools.

There have been Thieves before in our Land
when the Harvest Left Enough Surplus for the Thieving Hand
and the Thief Never Reaped Much More than Farm Owner

But the Harvest Dance is Gone
Our Harvest Gatherers Crawl on Empty Granary Floors
Picking Crumbs from Termite's Hope
Brushing Tears Away   Gathering Memories
        from Ashes in the Sand

        our People   Oh our People
        How Soon Again in our Hive
        Shall we Swarm Around our HoneyComb?

So the Thieving Hand has Reaped Much More
        than Farm Owner
and the Harvest Dream Transforms into Slow Funereal Hopes
the Rice Harvest has Gone to Weaverbird
the Corn-on-the-Cob has Gone to Grasscutter
the Yam-in-the-Mound was Carried off by Rat
and Now we Sit and Watch the Flowering Bean
and the Ripened Fruit of Palm being Plucked
at Dawn by Slippery Hands of Night Workers.

Tomorrow at Noon we'll Flock the Conference Hall
the Academy of Sciences. We will Hear the Learned Talk.
The New Guru and his Splendid Joke   the Post-Mortem
Expertise   the Learned Complex Talk upon

       Post-Harvest Perspiration of Yam Tubers
       the Who and the What Went All Wrong
       with What with Whom?

       Is it Enough   is it Enough to Dream
       the Moon and Stars
       When This Earth we Own we Can't Possess?

mr. poacherman

she don't live here no more
so don't you come here no more

they tells me how
there was shadows in my backyard
every time I goes to work at night
they also tells me how
always there was moanings from my windows
every time I goes away to the cottonfields

but she don't live here no more
so don't you come here no more

some folks   they likes to poach for love
they shoots arrows into virgin territories
they likes to scare some brother's joys away

poacherman   poacherman   please mr. poacherman
she don't live here no more
so don't you come here no no more

these days   brotherman
I sometimes stands me
at the corner of the train station
                the bus station
                the air station
I reads the arrivals board
for times I wish to come back from the past
But I sees only departure notices
of all those joys that flew away

at home at night at dawn at noon
all day all night
I folds my arms around
empty spaces in my life

I grabs at things ain't there no more
I sometimes catches only cobwebs in my dream

poacherman poacherman   please mr. poacherman
she don't live here no more
so don't you come here no no more

Sound and Silence

Because because I do not scream
You do not know how bad I hurt

Because because I do not kiss
          on public squares
You may not know how much I love

Because because I do not swear
          again and again and again
You wouldn't know how deep I care

You keep saying
How somehow our world must live by signs
But see how much we give away
Doing time in pursuit of signs
          deprived of all meaning
          and of all purpose
We break our words in two.   Then we
Split each half into Sounds and Silences

The News from Home

I have not come this far
        only to sit by the roadside
        and break into tears
I could have wept at home
        without a journey of several thorns

I have not spread my winds so wide
        only to be huddled into corners
        at the mere mention of storms

To those who hear of military coups
        and rumours of civil strife
        and bush fires and bad harvests at home
        and come to me looking for fears and tears
I must say I am tired
        very tired
        tired of all devotion to death and dying

I too have heard of
       all the bush fires
       the sudden deaths
       and fierce speeches
I have heard of
       all the empty market stalls
       the cooking pots all filled with ash and memory
And I am tired
       tired of all these noises of
       condolence from those who
       love to look upon the anger of the hungry
       nod their heads and stroll back home
       worrying and forever worrying
       about overweight and special diet for dogs and cats

Like an orphan stranded
       on dunghills of owners of earth
I shall keep my sorrows to myself
       folding them with infinite care
       corner upon corner
       taking pains the foldings draw circles
       around hidden spaces where still
       our hopes grow roots even
       in this hour of finite chaos

Those who sent their funeral clothes
        to the washer man
        awaiting the mortuary men to come
        bearing our corpse in large display
Let them wait for the next and next
        season only to see how well earthchildren
        grow fruit and even flower
        from rottenness of early morning dreams

Meanwhile
I am tired
tired of all crocodile condolence

        August 1, 1983

AKOS

You are the Mountain Dew … Falling ….
Up from EyeBrows of the Gods.

Flight Time

Have you Ever Sat on Air
            in an AeroPlane
& Found your Breath Caught
            Between Eternities?

Did you Ever Forever Think
            of how Swift the Winds
            may Come   and Blow
You Away to Ash and to Memory?

The Homing Call of Earth

So now I Come Back Home to Earth

I will remake my little Peace with Death
       sink my fingers deep and deeper still
       into this early morning dampness of our Soil

I'll take my sandals off
       plant my feet among these ashes
       left by the season's many brushfires

My skin again shall feel
       the wet nuisance of dawn and dew
I'll hurry me up those old bush paths
       down those farms where once there grew
       the foods on which we grew to life's fullness
       even in those times of storms

They say our land has lost her joys
to seasons of teething pains and aches
that stupid elders and wild hunters
took and hid our hopes in foreign caves
 and our offspring die of *kwashiorkoric* dreams

But against the distant gleam of shooting stars
I chose and will choose again and again
The Homing Call of Earth

I am EarthChild turned to Ghost
at festivals of MoonChildren
my steps uncertain trods on Alien Feet

There is no Sure Motion
          Except
In the Orbit of our Own Minds

So I must reject the honeyed call of distant dreams
And come back home to ragged hopes of Earth
The wealthy child's wardrobe may not outmatch
The earthy Elder's termite-eaten wooden box of rags

Our Earth survives recurring furies
          of her stomach pains and quakes
From the bleeding anger of her wounds
          volcanic ash becomes the hope
          that gives rebirth to Abundance of SeedTimes.

EarthChild

And Still we Stand so Tall   among the Cannonades
We Smell of Mists   and of Powdered Memories. . .

Born To Earth   and Of the Earth
      we Grew like Infant Corn among the Locust Clan
      we Gathered our Dawn in Armfuls of Dust
      we Blew BrainStorms in the Night of our Birth

Termites came and ate away Our Voice
      ate away our Rainbow's Gown of Flames
      Soiled Memories with Wild Banquets of Blood

And Still we Stand so Tall   among the Cannonades
We Smell of Mists   and of Powdered Memories

There once were Gods who came at Dawn
and took away our Voice
leaving here the howls of Storms
the screams of Devotees
the rancid breaths of Priests

But Still we Stand so Tall   among the Cannonades
We Smell of Mists   and of Powdered Memories

Seyam Sinaj   Sinaj Seyam   Seyam Sinaj
EarthChild   EarthChild   EarthChild
Sinaj Seyam   Seyam Sinaj   Sinaj Seyam

I am   you are   my song   our dream   your dawn
our love   our Hope
I Sought your Soul   you Sought my Soul so Long
in Cross-Rhythms of Jazz   in PolyRhythmic Miles of Jazz
till Miles   our Davis   led us through the Agonies of Joys
and Donny Hathaway   Checking Out so Soon   so Young   so Good
Walking Off with All his Stuff with Almost All our Song

I Lost   I Found you Again In Wails of SaxoPhones
Found   Lost you Again   to Rumbling Weight of Drums
Lost Found you Again in Hopeful Booms of God's Trombones
your Voice so Strained against the Pains the Ecstasies

      And Still we Stand so Tall   among the Cannonades
      We Smell of Mists   and of Scented Memories. . .

and yet Such Menace in Casual Glance of Friends
so much Fear in Eyes of MythMakers
some Swear there will be Mountains Washed Away to Sea
SeaGulls Flying Through our Whispered Dreams
Pains so Deep in GraniteWalls of Souls
CornCobs left Half-Burnt from Blazes in our Mind

      But Those who Took Away our Voice
          Are Now Surprised
      They Couldn't Take Away our Song

your Songs Traverse this Land of Hostile Winds
you Blow BrainStorms into BanquetHalls of MoonChildren
you Die   you Live   in Song
you Hate   you Love   in Song
you Measure our Joy in InterPlay of PolyRhythmic Sounds

Sinaj Seyam   Seyam Sinaj   Sinaj Seyam
Earthchild   Earthchild   Earthchild
Seyam Sinaj   Sinaj Seyam   Seyam Sinaj

I am   you are   my Song   our Dream   my Love   your Dawn
our Hope
You Sought my Soul   I Sought your Soul so Long
in Cross-Rhythms of Jazz   in PolyRhythmic Miles of Jazz
till Miles   our Davis   Led us Through the RumblingWeight
 of Drums
I Found   I Lost you Again   to Wails of SaxoPhones
Lost Found you Again in BoomingHopes of God's Trombones

And Still we Stand so Tall   among the Cannonades
We Smell of Mists   and of Scented Memories. . .

But come next Fall   EarthChild   EarthChild   EarthChild
I may Lose you Again to PamperedDreams of MythMakers
Lose you Again to ImperialDreams of History's PawnBrokers
and all I have is

        a Song for You
        a Song for You
        a Song for You. . .

You'll Walk Away with all our History Braided on your Head
all Woven into Cross-Rhythms of Hair   each Strand
so Linked to Every Other Strand   each Path
so Linked to Every Other Path   each Destiny
the Destiny of Every Other Single Destiny

And in All AlleyWays of Old London   and Paris   and Lisbon
And in All HarlemWays of New York   Chicago   New Orleans
in Kingston-Jamaica   Havana in Cuba   Atlanta in Georgia
on Voudoun Shores of Haiti   our Haiti   Oh Haiti!
on Voudoun Shores of Haiti   Oh Haiti   Our Haiti!
on Voudoun Shores of Haiti   our Haiti   Oh Haiti!
you'll Find FootPrints Running BackWays
into Lives once Lost to Sharp Rhythms of Panther's Greed
Lives All Lost to ColdEmbrace of Atlantic's Waves

EarthChild   EarthChild   EarthChild
Seyam Sinaj   Sinaj Seyam   Seyam Sinaj
EarthChild   EarthChild   EarthChild

I Sing   I Sing   I Sing
A Song   A hope   A Love

>   a Song for You
>   a Song for You
>   a Song for You

>   *And Still we Stand so Tall   among the Cannonades*
>   *We Smell of Mists   and of Powdered Memories. . .*

>   *And Those who Took Away our Voice*
>   *Are Now Surprised*
>   *They Couldn't Take Away our Song*

Selections from A HARVEST OF OUR DREAMS

Mythmaker

For George Dakpo   S O. Smith   Adjei Barima:They
Lost their lives in student risings against the Panther's Boast.

The Children are Away
The Children are Away
The Children
These Children are Away
Away in SchoolRooms where the World in Book
Distills DayDreams into Visions
Burns Memorials of the Past
in BonFires of the Soul

What shall we say to Mythmaker
When and If he comes?

Nothing.

He will come and find for himself
how our History Gathered Discarded Myths
from Peddlers of Rumours and Bearers of Tales
and with a Few Conjunctions of the Law
Constructed a New Constitution
for the Union of our Several Selves

The Children
These Children are
Away   Miles Away from Home
Plucking Poison Kisses from Laurels
Blooming with Rage in Mid-Winter.
Some Day they will be Home.

They will Turn and Return
with Garlands for their Land
But they will sigh to see how for Six Seasons
our Mothers Fed on New Dirges
our Common *Kenkey* Grown so Lean
we Needed a Decree to Insure her Health

our Scholars   Deployed from Campuses
into Ghost Communal Farms,
Walked the Streets at Dawn like Zombies
Peddling Posters Proclaiming Final Obsequies
for the Revolution that Went Astray…

They will be Hit by Stray Bullets
They will be Clubbed to Death in Dark Corners
And we will hear of Brass Band Processions
Congregating at our Castle of Despair
Celebrating the Victory of our Death…

The Children are Away
The Children are Away
The Children
These Children are
Away.
Some Day they will be Home
for Final Rites for the Late Renegades.
Their Garlands will pass for Wreaths.
And yet Somehow   they won't be Sad or Mad.
They will Turn and Return to a Bereaved Home
and Still they won't be Mad or Sad.

Though our Memory of Life now Boils
into Vapours   the Old Melody of Hope
Still Clings to Tenderness of Hearts
Locked in Caves of Stubborn Minds.

The Children will be Home
The Children will be Home
The Children
Those Children will

                    Be Home
                    Some Day.

                    Maamobi, Accra. 1 June 1977

SeedTime

Do not Search too Hard
for Words to Trap these Thoughts
the Thoughts that Bring the Tears
upon the Harvest of our Dreams

They say our Thoughts are Threads Crossing
and Criss-Crossing into New Cobwebs of Life
And
I shall Spin a Handful of Hopes
against this CutBack in our Dreams
against this Wild BackLash of Screams
even against these Lingering Doubts
at Testing Time for our Faith in Gods

We Load our Voice with These Burdens
Searching Myths for Miracle Drugs
Distant Cures for our Sickness of the Soul

This Land Survived the Flood of BirthWaters
but MoonMen came with Gifts of Thunder
so we Drank a Barrel of MoonShine
and Lost SeedTime in Seasons of Harvest Dance.

But SunGod comes to Claim his Own at Harvest Time.
At Heaven's Other Gate   a Friendly Soul Appears
Wearing a Gown of Velvet Flames:

> There is No Curse on Us
> he Sings
> There is No Curse on Us

We who Bought Fevers from PawnShops of the World
And Tread ByWays with Burdens in our Voice

> There is No Curse on Us
> There is No Curse on Us

Our Orphan Laid an Egg across the Backyard of the Skies
The RainStorm Came and Swept it all Away
Again he Laid an Egg across the Backyard of the Skies
Again the RainStorm Came and Swept it all Away
Today she Sows a Mystery Seed in Bosom of WhirlThoughts
Our Predator Birds shall have to Prey upon
Their Own Anger   Their Own Nightmares

     We will Not Die the Death of Dreams
     We will Not Die the Cruel Death of Dreams

There Will be Anthems Sung for Victories Reaped in Dreams

Our Harvest-Gatherers Crawl on Granary Floors
Poking Naked Fingers into Armpits of the Soul
and Laughter Comes Rolling Through our Voice of Tears
Weaving the Season's Final Dance for Miracle-Makers
and Now we Must Wear this Gown of Flames
and Walk on Stilts across Mirages
in these Deserts of our Soul
and Mythmaker shall Draw the Shrouds Apart
and There   in the Wake of Screams
we Embrace a Voice Wearing our Dreams

And So we Find the Voice to Trap These Thoughts
These Jogging Hopes for a Harvest of our Dreams

> There is No Curse on Us
> There is No Curse on Us

> We will Not Die the Death of Dreams
> We will Not Die the Cruel Death of Dreams

Bloomington, Indiana, 1-12 April 1972

A Harvest of Our Dreams

There is a Ghost
on Guard
at Memory's Door
Sscaring away these Pampered Hopes
these Spoiled Children of our Festive Days

The HoneyBee had Plans in Store
for his MotherQueen: He went Across the World
Gathering Fragrance from Dreamy WaterLilies
from Lonely Desert Blooms
Some Other Gatherer Came with Plans
all for his Own Desires
Our Hive Went Up in Flames.   I was Away.

      We will Hum a Dirge for a Burden of These Winds

Memories of our HoneyComb Floating Through
      SeedTime within the Soul beyond the Reach of Song
      Rowdy Echoes Burst Upon our Soul's Siesta

      And Harvests Go Ungathered in our Time

There will be Strange Voices Filling Spaces
in our Mind   Weaving Murmurings Upon
the Broken Tails of Songs Abandoned Once in Playing Fields
Rumblings from our Past are Planting Stakes
Across our New RainBows
and in Seasons of HarvestDance
there Still will be a Ghost
on Guard
at Memory's Door

It was For Shame the Turtle
Hid his Pain Beneath his Shell
and Crawled Upon the Pleasures of the Sea.
His Secret Pain became a Hidden Rottenness
a Poison to his Smiles

We will Hum a Dirge for a Burden of These Winds

Memories of our HoneyComb Floating Through
SeedTime within the Soul beyond the Reach of Song
Rowdy Echoes Burst Upon our Soul's Siesta

And Harvests Go Ungathered in our Time

So these Echoes Come in Ritual Dance
from Old HomeSteads where once She often Sang
Singing the Dirge   Keeping the Wake at Endless Funerals

> *Dɔtsa of the Sea   I am Dɔtsa of the Sea.*
> *I did not know it would be like this for me*
> *Yevu's Net has Caught Me with My Dreams*

And Now we Tread ByWays
Searching Passing Faces
for Fleeting Image after Image
Seeking Kindred Minds
for Lost PassWords into Fiestas of the Soul

Somehow   we Know the Carnival Days
Cannot be Gone so Soon
We may Gather Again Those
Unfinished Harvests of our Soul.
Uncle Demanya shall Come Back Home
with the Bread Basket of which
he Sang Through Life Across the Hunger of our Graves
Uncle Demanya shall Come Back Home
with the Bread Basket of which
he Sang Through Life Across the Hunger of our Graves.

Bloomington, 4 February - 1st April 1979

The Hyena's Hymn

For Obiba

They will come this way some day
these demigods with broken oaths
for a harvest of our dreams
They will come seeking lonely paths
through our famished dreams
to the house of exiled gods

I will make music with howls of dogs
I will borrow the shrieks of witches
the screeches of dancing monkeys
I will make music with howls of dogs

When the Christ strayed into
our village one shroudy Easter Dawn
our people took him for a ghost
It was not their fault: He was
standing upon the grave of a destooled chief
the chief who stole the diviner's oracle bag
and stole his children's bowl of soup
and pawned his oaths for a brief season of grace.
He had a monster child who died before the outdooring.

So when the pastor came dancing in
pursued by disciples selling hosayanas
Our people stood before the cemetery gates
reminding the gods to protect their children's
souls against these messengers of death.

I went into our Parliament Home
seeking audience with Speaker's Chair
They said I must have just returned from farm:
Parliament had gone on sudden leave
prior to retirement
They misdirected me to our Castle
where they gave me forms to fill
still standing at the gates.

I said I had a dream
to place before the military governor's
Boots--
I am a visionary   you know?
only so far   my visions have been
of things we didn't do   things we could have done.

They said our Castlemen were all dizzy
making grand visions from dreams of fallen gods
and in any case I was not properly dressed
and my name could not be found
in the register of co-opted councilmen

I pulled out my birthplace card
They said it had no official signature

I swear ma papa and ma mama born me
long long before they born them 'lectoral commissioner

They laughed. Yes   those sons of thugs and whores
They laughed and asked if
I wanted a noonday bowl of flames

They said I could give my dreams
to our birthplace dogs
or just dump them on the dunghill.

In absence of a Chief Justice
I File my Appeal at the Low Court of Memory

because I am ignored   because
because I am abandoned to my dreams
I lay ambush within my soul
preying upon prenatal doubts
nostalgias of my broken world

and if
they should come this way some day
those demigods with broken oaths
for a harvest of our dreams
if by some curse they should
come seeking those lonely paths through our famished dreams

I will make music with howls of dogs
embrace their groans with laughter from our wounds
flood their graves with hurricanes of our blotted joys.

I will borrow the shrieks of witches
the screeches of dancing monkeys

I will make music with howls of dogs.

Legon, 8 September 1977

The Diviner's Curse

again for Obiba

Your prayers   my people
are doing a dance of ghosts
upon the courtyard of my song
and I wake to meet
my voice running naked
across our house of storms

>   a diviner foretells a groan
>   beneath the joy of birthday feasts
>   a drunken brother drags the oracle bag
>   into a harvest bonfire
>   cowries scream above the roar of brushfires

I too wonder at the zeal of these prophets who
come offering half-truths for a harvest of our dreams
I marvel at the glory in their vision
the smile around the corners of their voice

I know some day they will be home
The children will come pointing questions at
Us.
Do we not welcome these prophets here
with communal ritual feasts
see them go with lips besmeared with he-goat fat?

The children will come pointing questions at
Us.
Here I stand mumbling apologies into my beard
I spend a fortune rehearsing
the lies we shall have to tell
to explain our manhood's failure in prime of youth.
I teach myself to be wily as the tongue
to move with craft among the knife-throwers

Thus I become a coward
to the courage of our thoughts

And the children shall come pointing questions at
Me.

Hohoe, 21 December 1977

AKƆFA

Blewuu

Blewuu… Blewuu… Akɔfa   Blewuuu…

Words are Birds: They fly so fast too far
for the hunter's aim. Words are Winds:
Sometimes they breeze gentle upon the smiles
our hearts may wear for joy. They fan the sweat
away from Fever's brow. They lull our minds
to sleep upon the soft breast of Earth.
Yet soon too soon words become the mad dreams
of storms: They howl through caves through joys
into shrines of ThunderBolts. They leave a Ghost
on Guard at Memory's Door. Therefore
gently…gently…Akɔfa, ge-nt-ly…
take care what images of life
your tongue may carve for show
at carnivals of weary Souls

Nunya

Ha … ha … ha … ha … ooo … yi!

Let me laugh a small laugh as though
my heart were doing a little dance of joy.
Your tongue   our brother   is a dawn breeze
spreading peace upon an orphan's fear for eyes
of day   but my mother's husband's youngest son
do not eat salt and give yourself heartburns.

I know you've seen the world through windows
in your school   and they say your view is sharp.
Yet you are only our little darling master.
I saw my moon in many many skies before
your sun first raised his head into our clouds.

Please   please   do not frown and sneer into my face.
I do not deny that even a child may have wisdom.
But the wisdom of the child is a piece of broken pot
in the sand. The toddler may claim it for his own
hold it to his bosom   and fight a duel to keep it still.
Yet for all his mad pleasure
it is only a broken piece.

This child owner of great treasure
what can he tell of what became
of the other broken pieces? How
could he tell the shape of the pot
that broke and lost the dreams it cooked
for how many feasts   for how many Moons?

And who could the porter be?

The head that first carried the image
of that pot   the hands which gave that image
to the world   what may have become of them?

So you see   my mother's master child?
There is no absolute knowledge
to the waywardness of life's byways.

These little cassava sticks of mine
have left their mark on several tracks of life.
But the thing I chased exchanged his feet for wings
and I am a hunter come home with a basketful
of wild tales of how it is today that the cooking pot
must sleep mouth-down in a corner of the old kitchen.

Dàdá

I remember how mother sat me down upon her thighs
and drank the joy from my eyes
her lips poised uncertain upon
the brim of a smile that never
once blossomed into wild petals of joy.

With the child's abundant faith in life
and a crowded world   I screamed
with mirth to teach her smile to bloom.

But now   with all these cracks in faith
behind mother's smile of joy of love
I see those stumps of joys
cut down in mid-season.

The pot in which she cooked her dreams
fell and broke in the sand   and she was searching
for lost childhoods on my beauty's dawn.

Tugbedzevi

I remember well the coming of that dawn.
How I woke up from the naughty sleep
of the carefree child and found
a gentle dream coiling on my bed
her head upon my bosom for a pillow.
I tied her well around my ripening waist
to hold my little passion cloth.
And when I stepped outside into the world beyond our house
I caught my beauty's dawn peeping over our fence
hiding behind the trees behind our house behind
the things that hide behind those shadows in our mind.

Still drowsy from my sleep I yawned
and stretched myself into a bow   and
arrows from my breasts shot into the dawn
and caught beauty weaving a pubertal dance
in a ritual feast of dream and dawn and hope.

And I remember well   yes I remember
But how can I forget all those early
morning joys   grumbling through the dew
to wake the river with our chattering
whispering teasing gossips about
the foolishness of boys who thought
their voice was grown quite big enough
to bear the weight of burdens they could give.

Sometimes too   we talked of funny old men
with the waist of the wasp. They kept asking
useless questions   sending boring greetings
to your parents   casting sly glances
at things too fresh for their souring tastes.

Tsitsa

And then of course we argued about teachers
those teachers in the school.   We all agreed
they really could be funny. I mean sometimes.

There was the big man Masita Matiasi himself.
They say he went to koledzi somewhere up
in the mountains of Amedzofe. Then he went again
to another koledzi   also up and up in the chain
mountains of old Akropong   or was it Abetifi?

Now I cannot even tell. Anyway   it was always
on mountains. So when he came down
to this village in the valley   his head was full of skies.

He talked about Mawu Yehowa without swallowing saliva.
May be Mawu was his Grand Father.

As for Inglishi   he could speak it better than Ako
Sometimes his pupils licked those bib big words
rolling down his tongue into his he-goat beard.
Sometimes too those rolling words fell down on his belly.
He had the belly of a toad and he always
talked pulling up his ancient trozasi.

Awoyo

Awoyo crossed my path and spat upon my toes.
I did not cough.
She went away strutting about
and stepped upon a thorn.
She came right back and spat into my face.
I did not even sneeze.
She shuffled away with a scowl on her evil face
hoping she was smiling.

I sit down here thinking she'll bring herself again.
I will slash her with my tongue
and spread hot pepper in her wounds.

The witch daughter with the face of an owl.
Awoyo   come back here and
I will sing to you your shame.
That night you went talking to
every stick and every little rope
swearing you caught Agbenɔxevi on top of me
doing some funny thing behind your smelly mother's
broken fence. You must have walked out
straight from a strange nightmare.

Come   Awoyo   come back here and
I will give it back to you   give to you
the thing Agbenɔxevi told you once
at a gathering of the youth.   He said
he would not take a hundred Awoyos.
Not even for a gift.   He said even if
your mother gives you a ritual bath on Christmas Day
if she covers up your nakedness with velvet cloth
and hangs diamond pearls about your stringy neck
and gives you away with a live turkey and eggs and all
He Agbenɔxevi would send you back at noon
to wherever you may have found your strange beauty.

Today for me is like your yesterday.
You're glad he's gone away from me.
But he will be back. I know he will be back.
Though now you cross my path and spit into my face.

You spread rumours I have no womb for birth   that
at my age I must begin to think of grandchildren.

Awoyo   I am not the whore's daughter like you
Your mother went from this village to that village
Shitting babies all along her path across the clan.

Did she ever suggest to you
Who your papa could have been?

They say the day she died the elders sighed
And poured a long libation on her grave
Praying her soul to come next time somewhat reformed.

You witch daughter with the face of an owl
Come cross my path again

I will spread your shame for you to crawl upon.

Fertility Game

In a public performance the opening line should be
repeated by the audience throughout the entire poem.

Come back Home   Agbenɔxevi   come back Home

A week today at carnival time
young men of the land will gather
for the wrestling duel of song and dance
maidens will sharpen their tongues and
carve praise images of dream lovers   and
I have a gourdful of praise names laid aside for you

Come back Home   Agbenɔxevi   come back Home

In the eyes of town
I will break the evil glance of witches
I will pour you a calabash of pride
I will hold it firm to your lips
till your eyes catch the gleam of stars
till your mind reaches out for moons
till your body vibrates to rhythms of the seas

Come back Home   Agbenɔxevi   come back Home

And your voice shall rise deep across the years
Through rainbow gates to beginnings of things
It will come floating through seasons of glory
thundering through deserts and pain fields
where our people died the death of droughts and of wars
where they died   and lived again
where they die   and wake up
with seeds of life sprouting from their graves

Come back Home   Agbenɔxevi   come back Home

Agbenɔxevi   Atsu Agbenɔxevi
I have held my passion in check for you
holding it fast against storms   against thunder
held it firm against the haunting smiles of gods.

I have strained my bosom against the sharp edges
of harmattan winds   against the rumbling weight
of May rainstorms.

I am the rainbow standing guard
across your path of storms.

Atsu   I have died a hundred deaths for you.
Each time each night   I wake up again and again
In that house we built upon the shores
With pools of troubled seas.

    Come back Home   Agbenɔxevi   come back Home

All   all my peers now carry big babies on their back.
Still   I carry mine in my heart.   Sometimes in my loins.
And O she cries so much for you.

    Come back Home   Agbenɔxevi   come back Home

Kokui   my young sister   went away last moon
the harvest time.   She swallowed a tiny gourd seed
so now she carries a giant gourd in her belly
for Senyo   our dying Chief's only living son.

Even Foli   my mother's youngest child
now speaks in the broken voice of a man-child.
They say at the village school he goes
pinching the bigger girls on their wosowosos.
They always scream but they never report him.
And once the teacher caught him
he explained oh it was only a little test
to hear the difference in voice pitches
of teenage girls and teenage and boys!

They let him off   and now he comes
boasting he's man enough
to handle a thousand meddling teachers.
He even talks to me of a swift madness
there may be in these words I give to the winds for you.

Come back Home   Agbenɔxevi   come back Home

I have woven a hundred songs for you   woven them
all into pillows for your wandering head of dreams.

For your bed   I plucked feathers from peacock's pride.
Each midnight moonlit night   I walk naked
to the crossroads towards the setting place of Sun
I lean against the firm bosom of our ancient baobab tree
I close my eyes   I give your name to westbound winds.

And in a careless abandon to joys there are in songs
I stretch my breast against the Moon's glory   just
waiting to dance you home to your rainbow bed
where you and I may wrestle again   all over again
in that Old Fertility Game first played by Gods
in the SeedTime of our Earth.

I say today I stand naked beneath our baobab tree
watching your dreams running along the path of storms.
I will woo you yet with glories of the Moon while
our hunters break their tongues in strange whispers
of Moon Deity at life's crossroads
keeping vigil for SunGod's homecoming
from ramblings across the skies
through Thunder's gates and lightening's path
Into house of fugitive dreams.

Come back Home   Agbenɔxevi   come back Home

Come with me to your rainbow bed
Where you and I shall wrestle again and again
All over again   in that Old Fertility Game
First played by Gods in the SeedTime of our Earth

Just come back Home   Agbenɔxevi   come back Home.

Hohoe, 28 February 1978—Bloomington, 21 November 1979

The Word

And so these worshipers of gorgon and moron
Came into his home. He was away
In cornfields rehearsing the rain dance
In wake of wandering clouds...

To his kids they whispered things. Gave them
Miracle drugs wrapped in arguments of sugar.
Gave them powdered milk in polythene bags.

He came back home with a harvest
of
corn-cobs and honeycombs.

His children met him
at the gates singing hosayanas.

Their mother   they said   had gone
to the next and next village
whispering
The Word.

Bloomington, 22 April 1979

Do not give too much of your love to me

Do not give too much of your love to me
I am the bird with voice of dreams
I bring the brief glory of wings upon the rays
Long ago   I chose the rainbow for my soul

I am
the bird in flight
the arrow through your night

Do not give too much of your love to me

Once the angels stole my cloth somewhere
upon the clouds in the house of storms
Today   I sweep the sky   I leave Footprints
On ThunderClouds
I spread the swift glory of wings upon the rays

O Do not give too much of your love to me

Bloomington, 14 April 1979

Murmuring

I met a tall broad chest
Strolling down deep night
with my fiancé in his arms

She passed me off for a third cousin
on her mama's side of a dried-up family tree

I nodded and walked away
murmuring unnamable things to myself

Legon, 10 May 1978

Old De Boy Kodzo:

I write you long long tam   I no dey hear from you.
I say me I go write you somting small again.

Dem tell me say you too you come for Varsity
Me I say tank Gods! Old De Boy too icome
for where dem say all de small peoplo
mas come and make dem big peoplo.
But lak I say som tam before de sodza peoplo
come bloody ma mauf   too much book
ino go make your pikin belly full.
But I sabe say your own concrete head
be too too fool.

Make you go hask Plofessor Kesedovo
Haskam say na which peoplo tief our corn?

First, igo tell you somting for som sakabo man
dem callam Kominizimu. Den igo tell you somting too
for som lie lie tiefman dem callam Demoklashi.
De big bookman go spiti im rotten salava for your face
and make som long long talk about cocloach and housefry.
Igo gib you somting dem callam Footunotu.

Na dis one go say:

 According to Disguintis Plofessor
   so so and so and so and so
 Accorling to meditasion espelmentasion and
   scienfitic consavasion invastigasion
 According to hleflence page so palaglaf so so and so
   articre one-and-half minus tree-one-qwata,
 Accorling to accorling and accorling...
   ibi akuko didi kakra.

Now make you hol im beard make you haskam
again:
   So Plofessor na which peoplo tief we na corn?

Igo smal kakra igo pull im beard igo say:
   To be continua…

O yah!   to be continua.

So we too we dey   and we go continua.
As for we   dem say we be simpel peoplo o
And so na how we go do?

Ah! Nye Bro   make I continua for you paa.

Na dis tam   dem tell me say
De zombi peoplo go take all dat useless cedi
Dem go trowam all for bola.

I say tank Gods!
Dem go trow all dem useless cedi for bola buuummm!
Den I say again O Gods Awuradi Nyankopong!
Why? Why you no collet all dees useless kalabule peoplo
And trow dem too for bola? Why O Gods? Why you let all
dees nyamanyama peoplo halahala ma people lak so?

Na God too I tink say idie long long tam ago ago.
Or lak idey for up   na im too perlaps go say:
          To be continua.

Wallahi! Tallahi! Bismillahi! Rrahmani-Rrahimi!

          Salaam aleikum
          Ibi mea. Your Vagabond Broda
          Kofi Abunuwas Abodzise.

They Hunt the Night

They have sought to put us away like
memories of a bad marriage of youth
But like wounds from naughty childhood days
We leave a perpetual scar upon
the forehead of their joy.

We are the dog who caught the game
but later sat beneath the table
over bones over droppings from the mouth.

In gentle tones the master talks of angels
coming down with gifts for God's children
Still we sing of ghosts who would not go to hell.

They hunt the night from cottage door to palace gate
knocking with boney skinny hands   scaring away
God's own children from playing fields at Heaven's
Gate.

So they seek to muzzle our howls   to chain our anguish
to their gates of hell. May be tomorrow they will
sweep us all into garbage cans with other testimonials
of their greed. But on wings of flames we'll rise and
float across their joys and rain rumours of blood
upon their festive dreams: Rumours   Dreams   Blood.

Bloomington, 15 October 1978

Long Distance Runner

From Frisco once
we drove across the wide yawn of the breezy bay
to the Oakland home of Mike who fixed
a memorial dinner for his years among our people
They call for song and I sing the story
of our wounds: the failures and betrayals
the broken oaths of war leaders grown smooth
with ease of civil joys

They laugh they clap they call for more

For a change   just for a little change   I sing
your dirge about their land's defeat in the beauty
of her dawn: the ghost of Harlem standing guard
across their bridge of mirth
their launching pad of dream and myth.

I sing also your long lament for grand Geronimo
Amerindian Chieftain who opened his heart a bit too wide
the lonely horseman who now perhaps only may be
still rides his old stallion across their dream their myth
forever riding his memory among mirages along eternities
reserved for him among snowfields spread across the breast
of the Earth   this Earth and all his Earth.

Halfway through your songs   I see the folly
and the wisdom of our choice in the cold stare
the shifting look in the eyes of our hosts   our very kind hosts

Who are we to throw back at a man the image of things
he strove so hard to burn to ashes in history's bonfires?

We know there is an agony in waiting for the Long Distance
Runner who Breaks
The Finisher's Line for the Judges to declare he

Jumped
The Starter's Gun

stepped upon some other runner's toes
threw him off balance and out the race

And what is a race   Cousin   without the rules
without other runners?

But leave him alone   leave him alone
to his glory looming large above his olive dreams.

Bloomington, Indiana. 23 November 1978.

Fugitive Dreams

Sons of the SunGod
we woo the Moon
along the frigid zones
of our fugitive dreams
seeking our night across
the backyard of the skies

They rode our dawn across
thornfields of the centuries
riding riding our memories
into snowstorms through
tornado bowls across
blizzards into caves of ice

They stripped us naked
in market place of gods
so now we wear our gown of flames
and spread mirages across
deserts and prairie fields
gathering the harvest
of their dreams into
snowballs for a game of peace of war
with Moonchildren on fields of storm
Still they ride   riding our rainbows
across graveyards and battlefields
of history's stupid wars
mythmaking our world from
wayward dreams of fallen gods

Let me borrow the voice of Silverman
and sing of mirages in these deserts of our Soul.

Bloomington, 11 October 1978

Renegade

From memory of the rioting mob
they hooked him out
for dishonourable mention in official bulletins
His name they nailed
to the upas tree on our public square

The crows will come and peck
At the vision in his eyes
But the harvest of his dreams
will not belong to the vampire

Our doves will come gather his words
into secret barns of souls
whose insurance against decrees of death
will not expire before the third coming

From hide outs in carnage groves
the vultures smell rumours
of blood flowing in open fields

They purge themselves against the feast of rot
But grief shall be the only testimonial for their greed.

Maamobi, Accra, 3 June 1977

Rush-Hour in Soul-City

Standing beneath your silk cotton at noon
I watch these little little ones
searching your village sands for lost pesewas
glancing across your empty market square
to the lean woman in noonday sun
selling hot beanstew with cold cornbread
and
from rush-hour in soul-city
memories come crowding through our world

Once upon a time at a point of time
and place in soul-city
we were whirlpools and whirlwinds and whirlthoughts
flooding earthspace and airspace and mindspace
we were voices and echoes and waves
weaving rainbows and rhythms across the twilight zone
we were dreams sending moonbeams
along time waves to other rainbows
standing guard at heaven's other gate.

It is rush-hour in soul-city
and on shores of eternity
ghosts are doing a ceremonial dance
at rebirth of new heroes

and here on earth we stand in flesh
to bargain with death over life's remnants
a widow sells cold cornbread
to outlive her husband's last harvest
an orphan searches sands for lost kobos
to kill the last hunger of youth

and still on shores of eternity
ghosts are doing a ceremonial dance
at rebirth of lost heroes
who
once upon a time at a point of time
and place in soul-city
were whirlthoughts and whirlwinds and whirlpools
flooding mindspace and airspace and earthspace
they were voices and echoes and soundwaves
weaving rainbows and rhythms across their twilight zone

We will again we will be dreams sending moonbeams
along timewaves to those rainbows
standing guard at heaven's other gate.

Hohoe, 1 January 1978

Sunbird

For Adele

They say the orphan may not die without
        a taste of harvest joys
Today your praise name laughs like west winds
        among our cottonfields
I found you in that walnut grove playing games
        with Moonchildren

Rainbows of Fall now play like glow worms
        in shadows of thunderstorms
You and I are grandchildren of SunGoddess
Here we stand naked in fields of snow
drinking pollen from breasts of shooting stars
But soon too soon my ticket will be here
and then I'll have to go

I may never find your voice among our harvest joys
But I'll search the songs of our people for echoes
of your laughter bursting through a million orgasms
        into Adamu's desecrated apple grove
My memory shall roll like sand dunes across those
cottonfields where once our Sunbird wove pillows
for the anguish of our Soul.
        Pay my Joy to John and Kay.

Bloomington, 14 November 1979

Selections from ELEGY FOR THE REVOLUTION

Libation

Aʋakpata-Aʋazoli   deliver me
deliver me across my joy
unto the kindness of the Vampire
My blood may quench her thirst for other souls
Let not this blood clot upon your love
I am strangling my joy within the bosom of your peace

The rotten soul of my festive years
is now an orphan to my bastard joy
My laughter congeals within the warmth
of my heart and Oh if Death were not but a myth
I could slaughter my Life upon your altars
This eternity of my penance
Torments the divinity of my soul
with the fierceness of noon madness

deliver me   deliver me
across my joy   unto the kindness of the Vampire.

Legon, 20 January 1977

My Last Testament

Adonú Adokli
Dancer-Extra-Ordinary
who threw dust into Master Drummer's eyes
so you've gone the way of flesh
danced on heels in a backwards
loop into the narrow termite home
Whatever befalls the panther in the jungle
The leopard would not forget about the hunt
The dreams we placed among the thorns
are still unhatched
Those debts we owe our orphan clan
are yet unpaid
and you—you—
Whatever befalls the leopard in his ambush
The panther could not betray the spirit of the hunt

Here at the haunted outskirts of life
I've crouched for a season
watching your rainbows dissolving into mist
Now I smell thunders
loading their cannons with furies of storms
my horizons grow blurred with
shivering images of all our old visions
a holocaust hangs upon the clouds
threatening remembrance of life's purpose
with a blank sheet of doubts
Now I gnash my teeth
bite my lips in a sudden resolve
to invoke grandfather's spirit name

Kátáko Gakó
Old Mad One says
he captured King Cobra's neck with naked hands
Yah! Kúmasí the Fearless Ghost
wrestles a soul from jaws of Death
Come, blood of spirits
Daze my eyes to fear
I toss these rising doubts to thunder
and stagger back into my soul, still
holding firm onto this growing confidence
this piece of our broken covenant
Whatever befalls the panther in the desert
The leopard would not forget the jungle war.

Legon, 16 November 1976

Oath Destiny

They perch upon the parapets   these renegade sons of our soil
Hurling profanities at the peddlers of decency
Pouring vulgarity into the council chambers of the moralists:

  You cover your rotten sores with borrowed
      velvet robes   coat your diseased teeth with
      stolen gold   and walk our corridors with
      the Bible on your tongue   selling the gospel
      for weekly collections of silver.

To
  whose dog did you give your shame   that
  you dare offer the holy sacrament
  with illicit wine and bread baked
  with corn swindled from our starving pagan peasants?

Your mouth you wash thrice a day   but
  your bowels you never purge   and
  our air stinks with the stench from your guts.

WE no longer can wait for the Second Coming
                              of YOUR Christ
Nor for the judgement day appointed
            by your God.

Chukwu has grown impatient with the unlimited
  patience of *Jehovah*   and can no longer
  await the pleasure of Jesus.

Before the High Council of the Supervising Deities
   of this soil of broken oaths and widowed virgins
   we summon you
We the little great-great-grand-children of
   Oduduwa and *Obatala*
   we charge you
   charge you with innumerable counts
   of despoiling our virgins and killing our little joys
   we challenge you

By all the thunders of *Xebieso*
By all the incurable infirmities of *Sakpana*
We swear to post copies of the Judgement
   to your God   Who is at Heaven
   Whose address we shall look up
   in the opening chapters of the
   Holy Bible   Unrevised Version.

Back to Memory

> running away from memory
> searching for reasons to die

You will go and come   come and go
hoping to break these chains of life
but your renegade mind will ride
your degenerate flesh across
fields littered with corpses of dreams
you dreamt once upon a hope
when the soul's desires burst in
upon strongholds of Hell   blew out
hellfire with a breath of mirth
long before the flash of lighting
smote down hellgate   letting loose
the thousand fiends that today
you pursue across deserts and battlefields
sending your mind

> running away from memory
> searching for reasons to die

The searchlights of your mind's day—
dreams are trapped by long shadows
of life   shoved off the cliff of memories
your paralysed soul somersaults onto
rubber rocks that bounce you back to life

       and you will mount the clouds
       to the house of storms where
       guardian demons relieve the mind
       of its useless burden of death

They will send you back to memory
Make you rich with reasons not to die

            Legon, 6-7 March 1976

Soul in Birthwaters

Suite for the revolution

Our Birth-Cord

    a piece of a meat lost in cabbage stew
    it will be found   it will be found

If we must die at birth   pray
we return with our birth-cord still uncut
our oneness with Earth undefiled

Last night on the village square a man
bumped into my conscience and cursed
our God. I refused to retort, knowing
how hard it is for man to wake a man
from false slumber
Our conscience would not be hurt
by threats of lunatics

    a pinch of salt lost in cabbage stew
    it will be found   the tongue will feel out

we heard their cries but thought of dogs
and ghosts. Ghosts gone mad at dogs
who would not give our village a chance
to sleep   to dream
Now they say we have to die
These brand-new men gone slightly drunk
on public wine   they say we have to die

163

Yet if we must die at birth   pray
we return with our birth-cord still uncut
our name still to be found in the book of souls
Across the memory of a thousand agonies
our death shall gallop into conference hall of a million hopes
a lone delegate at reshuffling of destinies

　　　　a piece of hope lost in public tears
　　　　it will be found   it will be found

And if we must die at birth   pray
we return with—
But we were not born to be killed
by threats of lunatics
The maimed panther is no playmate for antelopes

　　　　　　　　　　　　　　12 August 1975

Radio Revolution

Again this dawn our Radio
broke off the vital end of sleep

Revolution!. . .Devolution!. . . Resolution!

grab a razor-sharp machete
and step onto the paths of war

Across our yard   I disturbed a courtship
of the dogs. They barked and backed away

through streets to all familiar walks
through maze of slums to armed barracks
of peace. Where? Where?
old peasant with hoe in hand   I
seek Revolution. Where is Revolution?
young veteran with blood across blue eyes   I
knew of no Revolution   but I
met revolt limping down this road
chased by a howling herd of armed jackals

down this road   down this road
to the market square where an only
pig searching for a morning meal
took me for a moving lump of flesh
and charged at me   charged at me
with fangs sharpened by hunger's despair

I slashed her into two   wiped her
blood upon
                    her head

down this road   down this road
to Dependence Square seeking Revolution
I found a lone symbol for Peace
a nameless bronze warrior with empty
gun pointing Earthwards doing homage
to Earth Goddess

The school-boy newspeddler leans against
a smile   tells of how he came and found my doors
open   my inner rooms unguarded in the dawn

I was out my dear
I was out seeking Revolution

Our Revolution, Sir?   It's here in these
dailies.   The headlines display it:

THE REVOLUTION—NOT A CONCERT PARTY

The photograph confirms it:

Statesmen at State Banquets
Proposing a toast to the health of state:

LONG LEAVE THE REVOLUTION!!!

Legon, 5-7 March 1976

167

Soweto

let us accept the curse prescribed
by the good old lord
preach it a 1000 times
according to lessons read
by voices in the whirlwind

gospel confronts gospel
high-tension power-line
connects their various truths
the preacher creates a new
Gospel According to His Needs

we will make heroes out of street boys
train felons into statesmen

now world assemblies deal in lies
let us recruit liars for diplomats

Legon, 29 September 1976

HouseBoy

a young revolutionary lays ambush in my thoughts
firing sound bombs
into colonial barricades

my memory bumps
into the silence of
his 70-year-old
HouseBoy
he serves champagne in panelled living rooms
retreats at night to a toy
mud-hut with a bamboo bed
swallows a glass of liquid flames
turns his dreams loose
upon his private agonies

The dreams of Fanon's Wretched of the Earth
condense into storms in our morning sky
and
The burden of our guilt
hangs heavy upon our harvest joys

old memories discharge poison
arrows into banquet
halls where invalid souls
gather   celebrating a treaty
of peace between aggrieved conscience
and crimes against the self

Legon, 29 September 1976

Ghosts

a thousand ghosts haunt our soul in birth waters
this life would drown in blood
hammer falls on anvil
of this head   calabash cracks
scattering braindrops on pathways
offering a broken tale to passers-by

watch revolutions of worlds
load guts of goats with power
of bulls   the fools we were
we would seek refuge on wings of their visions
deserting the dream we placed among the thorns

they stole our sleep in a daylight siege
and in our brief madness
we exchanged lullabies for anguished cries

we were all away on the farm
when prowlers of night
sneaked into our pillows
oh   they would ambush our sleep
and strangle our dream

the vampires!   I saw them
they know I saw them when
father sent me home to fetch a little salt

My voice   my voice   they seek after my voice!
Do not put me to sleep   my people.

Legon, 31 December 1976

Dogs

The nose once said to the ear
all I ask of life
is just a little breath

Madman in the market-place
Let me be
only a madman in your market-place

I would howl and howl all day
but only to remind these
ghosts you're supposed to be in hell

Some people are cursing my dogs
for
howling through their sleep
How would they know
of
strange shadows
prowling among their sheep?

Legon, 31 December 1976

Elegy for the Revolution

a feverish psyche gropes for an
eye in shrines of Xebieso
the armoured hope lies exposed
to wrath of Thunderbolts

>These feet have kissed the sands of many shores
>Today they lay in cramps   crushed by revolving
>wheels of State
>This heart has felt the warmth of love   throbbed
>to beats of a thousand joys let loose upon a festive
>world
>Today it is a husk of corn blown before the burning
> grass

The Revolution violates a devotee   Beware
Beware the wrath of Thunderbolts
The agonised thoughts of a detainee translate
our new blunders into nightmares of blood & sweat:

>whips slashing through tender skins   broken bones
>collapsing to floors of cells   tortured moans
>bursting through concrete walls
>tearing through clouds and skies

>They seek refuge in house of storms
>and a sad conscience clears a path
>for poison arrows of gods of wrath

From sheltered yards of our righteousness
we watched the loading of an atom bomb
with a doubt on our lips   our cheeks
still blown with mirth of nights of revelry
our drunken ease forgetful of speed of light and sound:

       the muzzled heat of Hiroshima bursts into
       sudden flames   burns our laughter
       into screams   our crippled mirth wades
       through streams of blood   groping for memories
       of feasts flowing down turbulent gulfs
       half-filled with discarded blue-prints
       for a revolution gone astray
       into arms of dream merchants.

                    Legon, 28 February 1976

Dance of Death

Let us celebrate our
death by firing squads

To beats of martial strains
let us link our arms
on these public fields of blood
teach our feet to do the dance of death

Now there is still
some laughter in our souls
our feet with skill
will teach our pride to do the dance of death

The birth of a new nation
calls for sacrifice of souls
and our hearts are filled with
a passion for life by baptism of death

The growls of lions
are muffled by mumblings of thunder
The poise of panthers
baffled by flashes of flaming skies
The antelope passes through
on its peace mission to the little stream of life

Our minds have laboured in vain
preparing blue-prints for revolutions of peace

In this final hour of our triumph
let us celebrate our
death by firing squads

On these public fields of blood
let us link our arms
and teach our feet to do the dance of death

It is at the place of the dance
that elbow meets elbow
It is on the field of execution
that death embraces life
This is our ritual celebration
of marriage of death to life
The throb of mortal hearts
prepare our feet for the dance of cosmic love
The dance of death is a dance of grace
Put the rhythm to the loom
Weave new tapestries for our gliding feet
This rhythm grows too urgent for our peace
splitting our souls among a thousand desperate loves.

The dance of death is a dance of grace
Give us back those old drummers
Give them back those broken drums with nasal twangs
Call them here   call the owners of our town
Bring them stools to sit in state and watch
our feet in this final glide across our twilight zone

The birth of a new world
demands a little sacrifice of souls
and our hearts are filled with
a passion for life by baptism of death

The god of creation rambles
through the ruins of broken worlds
and
The process of reconstruction
is also
A process of demolition

Wheta, 4-11 September 1976

New Birth-Cords

You sit searching raindrops
for tears of thunder gods
harvesting shooting stars
in hope to rebuild comets
that strayed into uncharted milky-ways

You detain trade winds and bargain
for purified curses of rebel deities

That cloudy noon before
joy-maker's brief madness
say   that mid-day night
when you stood upon the banks of our humanity
and peered into our soul
what was it you saw
what indeed did you see
that today you are a ghost
haunted by crippling memoirs of years
and tears ago   unmoved by vows of rebirth
and oaths to weave new birth-cords
into honeymoons of coming resurrections?

Mean souls   unable to bear
the bruise of life's strictures
snatch at false deaths built of flimsy martyrdoms

Are you one of these?
seeking to make of your soul a sacrificial
sheep on the defiled altar of a nation's dreams?

The world   our world   is not worth dying for

a life is dearer than a wreath of tears
a nation may lay for a soul

All this talk of redeemers and sacrifice
of souls is a trap by rogues
a mesh to ensure unwary souls
do them in for extra days of joy

Do not   brother   die for a myth

                    Legon, December 1975

Taflatse

I vowed I would not offend the ears of decent folk
But now   Sadzi   you've fed my thoughts with gall
My song will be the great whirlwind
that snatches your only decent cloth
sells your shame to inner thoughts of men

The devil's oath you swore
to defame my name
undo the fame I wove around my neck
with years of honest toil

O Sadzi   Sadzi Dzisavi   so
you would be the unforeseen landslide
that comes to dislodge the ancient rock
on which I sun my higher thoughts
You would undo my fame?

But you Sadzi   you're yet to retrieve
the only underpants you ever wore in life
You pawned it years ago
for Paulie's pot of *tsukutsu*
And you want to undo my fame?

I Kɔdzo Kabaɖa   the evil
rope that binds   binding things that would not
be bound   binds the very things which
slip from hold of chains and copper wires
I'll bind your several shames
bind them tight with gentle
chords of my boundless song
sell your name in the market-place at noon

This dawn   I met a young virgin in
Tears   calling the clan to come witness
her woe.   O Sadzi   Sadzi Dzisavi   to whose
dog did you give your
shame   you dare attempt
a rape in a public
lavatory?

God   I hear   never had the chance to polish you up
You ran away half-formed   haunting the world
playing the truant to eternity

Sadzi   you're the evil
babe who pulled at the heartstrings of a sad
Mother. She died labouring to throw you out

And your father exchanged his manliness
for an eternity of shame
Today he walks the village lanes alone
eyes glued to his guilt   quietly keeping
distance from all women: no other of
your kind

And ah Sadzi   where is your sister now
who once upon a time strolled our lanes
with the easy poise of a natural queen?
They say she fled at night to Hausaland
leaving behind a big burden of shame
and rumour says she's now
mother to your child

This monstrosity of yours   Sadzi
Could this too be a gift of *Sê*?

Legon, 26 April 1976

Dance of the Hunchback

Mine is the dance of the hunchback
Along these quiet drains of town
I crawl my way with strain and shame
I leave paved streets to owners of the earth

He died.   Mother's other only son.   He died.
They said the doctor said
he died of innate poverty

Kinsmen came from distant quests
with precious things for parting gifts
pairs of velvet robes   diamond rings
a glass coffin with rims of gold
cases of schnapps   barrels of gun-powder
Each kind kinsman stood tall in our heart

an elder clears his ancient
throat   looks at me with loud
Silence
I ignore the threat in his eye

Going down on knees
I whisper my brother's spirit name
I whisper it thrice and offer all
I have: a Tear and a Song

At the wake-keeping this night
a cousin poet sells my shame in song

> a chief-mourner has laid a plot
> for a pauper's funeral
> kinsmen are not in it
> we weep this father
> whose line death snatches
> from an only proper son
> gives to a cripple to drag in dust

Public squares broad highways
and busy streets of town
I leave them all to owners of our earth
I crawl along quiet side-walks of life
With the hedge-hog and the crab
I carry a tedious destiny

Mine is the dance of the hunchback
In the valley behind my hill of shame
I do my best to fall in step
with rhythms of grace and pomp

But the eyes of the world
see only a moving bundle of fun
and upon my chest they heap
a growing burden of scorn

Wheta, 3 October 1976

The Last Dinner

I am the helpless fish
frying in your bowl of cooking oil
You lean against your kitchen wall
smiling with thoughts of coming feasts
But nature in time will call
You'll render accounts squatting on your heels
Your hunger returns with new demands
and I'll not be there
to feed the needs
of recurrent appetite

A Piece of Hope

I have searched the waves at dawn
for broken images of
the world we built upon the shores
with pools of troubled seas

The floods have gone to
where only storms may dwell
the beaches grown drowsy
sunning their naked breasts
amid murmurings of a million silences

I would rebuild our laughter
with echoes of the past
sleep at noon on remembered shores
dream of
doves perched on clouds across your milky-way

I would search the skies for new Edens
retrieve your voice from melodies of the spheres

The dolphins came riding the waves
a mermaid on their shoulders
She was casting your name upon the seas
whispering your laughter to the winds
They sat in the sand
purged my heart with a dirge   gave me
a piece of hope:
They will send you back some day

So now I search the waves at dawn
for broken images of
the world we built upon the shores
with pools of troubled seas

I would rebuild our laughter
with echoes of the past
dream at noon on forgotten shores
think of
souls asleep on moonbeams across my galaxy

I would search the skies for new Edens
reclaim your smile from Rainbows in my Soul

Wheta, 11 September 1976

Festival of Hopes

3rd Cock-crow

In the centre, where the midnight libation still lay in dregs,
a pointed peg broke through the soil   stood a foot above
the Earth.

Upon
this peg   a needle perched.
Upon
that needle   a calabash came and sat.
Inside
this calabash   there was a void.
Then the Clan appeared.
Around the grounds they threw a ring
their jaws still locked in a 7-day communion with Silence.
One by One
Man by Woman
Woman by Man
they stepped into the ring   bowed.
Publicly   silently   they shed their private fears
draining their secret cares
into that big brown calabash   Container of the Clan's Tears.

Noon

A step away from the calabash of public fears
Earth cracked and produced a neck without a head
the neck rose and revealed a body slightly pregnant
the body produced no legs: on a flat bottom it sat:
a Gourd.
Inside
that Gourd   there was a void.
Again the clan came
Around the Gourd   they wove a ring
their teeth still clenched in a cruel duel with Life.
Two by Two
Man and Wife
Widow and Orphan
they hopped into the ring   bowed.
Quietly   openly   they poured out their secret toils
draining their private sweat
into the deep brown Gourd pregnant with the Clan's Broils.

Dusk

3 steps from the Calabash of Tears and Gourd of Toils
the Earth pushed up a hearth.
Into
this hearth   dried wood piled up.
Upon
that pile   a pot installed herself
Inside
this iron pot   there was a void.

Screaming and shrieking and groaning and moaning
armed with muscle bone and nerve
eyes swimming in flooded passions of souls possessed
the Clan rushed   charged   stopped.

In the gathering dusk of that festive eve
each clansmanwoman gnashed his teeth
        and bit her lips
                and vomited blood
                 into
                 the void which filled that pot.

Upon no signal   the chant began: low   heavy   nostalgic
a terrible valediction offered in memoriam to a suspended
    millennium

Echoes   they say   fly fast to closed chapters of life
stirring frozen heartbeats of older worlds.

The chants rose deep mingling with
re-awakened rhythms of *atrikpui* and *adzogbo*
bringing vigorous memories
of mortalised heroes
and
ethnic vendettas.

The rhythms boiled to a frenzy   driving
Clansmenwomen crazy with re-juvenated glories
of younger worlds.

A clap of clouds   a shaft of light
and a distraught meteor struck the pile of wood
inflaming the hearth   the flames engulfing the pot of blood,
flooding the festive grounds with a glory
made hoary by crazed shadows of dazed clansmenwomen
each wrestling with a mortal self
in jubilant desperation to evoke the second self.

The flames made a triple leap and grabbed
the Gourd of Sweat and Calabash of Tears.
Excitement seized an old clansman—he tossed
himself above the flames and landed neat
                              in the pot of boiling blood.

He died chanting an ancient song of Life

The Clan forgot the chorus.
But they jumped and danced
embracing and shaking hands
                    watching the flames
                    dwindling into
                    a pencil
                    of smoke
                    which
                    shot
                    in-
                    to
                    higher realms   laden with
                    evaporated impurities for a symbolic
                    Purification in Distilleries of Destiny.

                    27 January—11 April 1976

Selections from BRAIN SURGERY

MY SONG[4]

Here
on
this
Public
Square
I
Stand

I Sell My Song for those with ears to buy
It is to a tree that a bull is tied
You do not bypass the palm's branches
        to tap its wine

The things I have to say
I say them now
        I shall stand aside
        for those who care
        to clear their throats and
        dress their shame in lies

When you meet a poorly-dressed neighbour
        at a great durbar
        you do not spit on the ground
        and roll your eyes to the skies

---

4 This poem is something of a signature tune, an invitation to "My Song." It is
in part a translation of, and in part an elaboration on, an original Ewe song by
one of the poet-cantors of the **Haikotu** Drum Club of my birth-place, Wheta.

The umbrella I bought
You stole it from my rooms at dawn
Now I walk in the early morning rain
You point at me to our young maidens
And they join you in laughter

Think
        My People
Think

Think well before you laugh at those who walk in the rain.

The gifts that Se bestows at birth
        Some had some splendid things
        What was mine?
        I sing. They laugh.
                Still I sell My Song
                for those with ears to buy

My cloth is torn   I know
But I shall learn to wear it well

My voice is hoarse   I know
But I shall learn to weave it well.

AGBAYIZA

Unpack your things
        Agbayiza
Unpack your things

The men who went before
        There they come
        with funereal faces
        still
        mourning the memory
        of
        those early dreams that
        died
        before the last cockcrow

Unroll your mat
        Agbayiza
Unroll your mat

        Let's lie down here
        and
        fix a date for Grandfather's funeral
        His curse we will remove
        and
        slumber in the shadow of his Soul

They who went before
        There they come
        with bloodshot eyes

        . . . Let us unpack our things. . .

They sold their farms
        and went away
        to fight for higher things

        . . .and guard our land. . .

Now they come
        with
        sorrow in their hearts

        . . . re-roof our farm houses. . .

They left us here
        and went away
        to
        feast on turkey tails

        . . . and clean our cooking pots. . .

Now they come

        . . . prepare our palm-nut soup. . .

Their bellies filled

. . . and pound our own fufu. . .

with sour memories
of
many a State Banquet
to
which they were never invited

Agbayiza

>Let us renew our Vows
>and
>Watch over our House

Those who break faith with their Gods
Go and come back without their Souls.

THE SONG OF A TWIN BROTHER
to Kofi Awoonor

Stand unshod upon the terrazzo floors of your balcony
Look over the barricade
       to the savanna grasslands of your countryside
Silence the stereo soundz of your radiogram
Open your Soul
       to the mellow tones of your country brother's xylophone

      So many Moons ago
      Before our world grew old
      I had a Twin Brother
      We sucked the same Breast
      Walked this same Earth
      But dreamt of worlds apart

And here I am today
Holding on to Grandfather's sinking boat
While Atsu my Twin Brother
Floats on air in Jumbo Jets
And stares into the skies
And dreams of foreign ports

Atsu e e e!
Atsu e e e!

Do not forget the back without which there is no front

Dada is still alive but grown silent
And full of songs sung in a voice
That hints of a heart overstrained
With the burdens of a clan without Elders

Our roof is now a sieve   Atsu
The rains beat us   Beat us
Even in our dreams
And the Gods they say are not to blame.

The State Farms have burnt the thatch and dug its roots
They grow rice.   And cane sugar
       But Oh!   Atsu
       My Twin Brother   Atsu!
       Our bowels are not made for the tasty things of life.
       The rice   the sugar   all go to Accra
       For people with clean stomachs and silver teeth
       To eat and expand in their borrowed glory.

Atsu e e e!
Atsu e e e!

>I shall give your name to the winds.
>They will roam the world for you.

You forget

>Atsu   my father's former son
>You forget the back without which there is no front.

Papa has lost his war against hernia.
Seven Keta market days ago
We gave him back to the soil
And Dada is full of *Nyayito* songs
sorrowing songs sung in a voice whose echoes
float into the mourning chambers of our soul.

Danyevi leeee!

>Dada says
>The tasty things of life are good
>But
>You do not chase Fortune beyond the point
>Where Old Sky bends down to have a word with Earth.
>You do not bury your arm in Fortune's Hole

There have been others before   Atsu
There have been others before you.

Armattoe went away
        Came   and went again
        Then he never came
Katako too went away
        Came   and went again
        Then *he* came. But without his soul.

Atsu

        I sit under this Oak where you and I once sat
        and cast cowries in the sand.
        I close my eyes. I give your name to the winds
        They will roam the world and find your ears.

Fo*f*onyevi leeee!

        Papa has gone to *Tsyiefe*
        Dàdá is full of *Nyayito* songs
        And I   Etse   your Twin Brother
        My heart overflows with unsung dirges.

        Many   many Moons ago
        Before the Silence came
        I had a Twin Brother.

        We shared the same Mat
        But parted in our Dreams.

AGBENƆXEVI

Agbenɔxevi!   Agbenɔxevi!!

I met you in a midday dream
You carried our sorrow on your face
And would not return my smile

Good Day! I said to you
Fires and Storms! you cried:

> Save him   some divinities   save him.
> Looking so sadly gay
> Attempting to sell the whiteness of his teeth
> While all around   the narrow lanes of life
> Are littered with half-dead bodies of brave kinsmen
> Who but a week ago stood firm on this soil
> Against the harsh treatments of a callous godfather.

> Wake him   some divinities   wake him up to hear
> How out of tune it is to sing Good Day to folks
> Who leap out of their midnight dreams
> To find their home on fire!!
> With flame and smoke all mixed up
> In one cruel consuming conflagration.

I closed one eye
        Agbenoxevi
I say I closed one eye and looked at you
My ill-timed smile half-dead upon my trembling lips

But But is it not true they say
that
Men do smoke even with gunpowder kegs upon their heads?

> True True very True
> But only with men who knew the direction of the wind
> Men who learned to keep gunpowder kegs
> Away from sparks of fire. . .

But But is it not truly said
that
Men do sleep in spite of Death?

> True True really True
> But only with men who knew the meeting point
> Of Sleep and Death. . .

Ah! But surely Agbenɔxevi surely
Unless the Bird dies young
Its feathers must grow Some Day!

A DIRGE FOR OUR BIRTH

Let us not ignore the testimony
        of our own misdeeds
and impair our reasoning
        with a stupid reliance
        on prophecies
        of these new Seers

In the early days of the craze
        for negation of our Past
did we not buy a coffin and celebrated the burial
        of a Brother who still walked
        this Earth with us?
did we not burn his barn and allowed a clown
        to rape his wife
        before our very eyes?

What fate befell the Child implanted in her womb?
Did we not refuse to attend the ceremony of his Birth?
And when he died so young of *kwashiorkor*
        how many wept for him?

Who can tell where they are today?
       the old priestess
       who read our future in a calabash
       the unhappy poet
       who composed a Dirge
       for the ceremony of our Birth?

Did we not twist their jaws
       and drove them
       beyond the boundaries of our dreams?

Now   we ask our mothers to confirm
       the things our grandmothers say.

We beg our children to tell us who we were.

GO TELL JESUS
to Koku

Go
Go tell Jesus
that his messengers have come
but have forgotten all His words
Ask Him if He said
Men are all equal or
Men are *un*-equal?
Who did He say God is?
A bearded old boogy
sitting far up in the skies
watching and not caring?

Go
Go ask Jesus
whether He really said
we cannot reach our God
if we do not pass through Him
Tell Him to tell you
 the fate of my ancestors
Who lived and died before
He the Christ was born
Will all of them be
Damned?

Go
Go ask Jesus
why He did not tour the world
to spread the word of death
but gave it to a chosen few

and in parables thy can't explain
Tell Him
Tell Jesus
that the little peace I enjoyed
before His messengers arrived
has been disturbed
and I cannot sleep and dream
until it is restored
Tell Him
Tell Jesus
there is chaos in my house
My sons have left their heads and hearts
My daughters their hearts and heads
They are screaming shrieking
burning each other's Souls
all because
His Messengers have come
but have forgotten His words
May it please Him come again
That we may see the truth
That the truth may make us see
That peace is not a piece of bread in wine

Go
Go tell Jesus
His messengers have come
But have forgotten His Words of Life

BRAIN SURGERY

Within
      the hazy memories
      of dazed companions
      there still waver
      blurred images
      of
      fertile years
      that
      turned arid
      at
      the prophesied clash
      with yelling vandals
      who
      sought to upset the old zodiac . . .

Within
      the sacred gloom
      of
      the Oracle of the Caves
      a trembling *Ɔkɔmfoɔ*
      pours out troubled incantations
      over
      a greedy fire
      into which
      he soon will throw
      the last seedlings
      of
      the only herbs that cure madness

Inside
     the Conference Hall
     of
     the white State House
     there sleep files and files
     of
     many a splendid scheme
     against
     the messengers of death
     Files. Only files
     And
     Microphones
     through which
     blessed blasphemies
     from mouths of saints
     run relays
     to
     hidden amplifiers in house of Gods . . .

The Master Architects
     of proposed pillars of state
     they have all retired
     into
     the Banquet Hall
     Echoes of their happiness
     steal down the evening breeze
     into
     the very lungs
     of
     the lost fishermen
     whose boat has just been washed ashore
     by the unkind permission of the god of storm . . .

Lying naked
>upon the operation table
>is
>the chloroformed body
>of Nana Africana . . .

Bending over him
>are the reverend figures
>of
>three Master Brain Surgeons:
>the first suffers from fits of forgetfulness
>the second they say is a retired drunkard
>the third a natural clown of first rate rank
>Together they are
>Supreme Judges of Sanity . . .

The Brain Surgery is performed:
>Nana Africana's mind
>>they declare
>is out of date
>They say he has chronic
>>psychedislocation
>and burns up his soul
>>in morbid melancholia
>all because
>Today would not be Yesterday
>Their tools for brain transplant
>>are yet to come
>Nana's mind cannot be repaired. Die he must . . .

We shall watch and wait   Novi
We shall wait and watch our mental fog to clear
When Nana goes to Breman
We shall hold back our tears
We shall bold back our fears
        and do a public post-mortem
Then perhaps we can perform
        a pre-mortem autopsy
        on
        These Master Brain Surgeons!

SHATTERED DREAMS

You promised us roof tops
Where we could sit and feel like Gods
We helped to build the roof
You offered to teach us how to climb
We pushed you up to tops
Now you won't come down to let us go
The ladder too you've taken with you
We cannot reach you with a leap

We have been waiting for too long
you have shattered all our dreams
And given us nightmares

      Patapaa   we are watching you
      Baba   we are watching you
      We say we are watching you
      And the Gods are watching too . . .

You spoke of super jumbo jets
that could take us to distant lands
We gave up half our wealth
You offered to teach us how to fly
We saw you fly away
Now you won't come down for us to go
Our passports too we cannot get
And people don't fly without a pass
We have been watching for too long
You have shattered all our dreams
And given us nightmares

Patapaa   we are waiting for our turn
Baba   we are waiting for our turn
We say we are waiting for our turn
We want to have our turn . . .

Remember the years we spent on Grandfather's land:
Planting harvesting sharing all the climates offered us
Remember the nights we spent by Grandmother's fire:
Singing listening telling stories the Elders bequeathed to us
Remember the oaths we took   the Gods we swore them by
We say remember those days before our dreams
      When you first told us about your dreams
Remember the misgivings we expressed
      then the arguments you used
      the references you made
      the comparisons you drew
      the conclusions you reached
      They seemed so convincing
      your dreams became our dreams

We say in the days before your dreams
We knew not of roof tops nor of super jumbo jets
And we had no need for them
But ever since you gave us dreams to dream
Yes   ever since your dreams became our dreams
We want to climb to tops
        to fly to distant lands
And we are watching   waiting for our turn

You promised us roof tops
You spoke of super jumbo jets
We helped to build the roof
We gave up half our wealth
And you have shattered all and all our dreams

Patapaa   we are watching you
Baba   we are waiting for our turn
Remember we are still waiting for our turn
You have been flying for too long!

FIRE
for Kofi Agovi

She found me basking in the Sun
lying on the shore with an oyster in my lap

      "Get up for the children's sake!
      The thick rain clouds on fire
      Your family house in flames
            and here you are
      Talking poetry to a mere oyster!"

      "But this oyster here tells me
      The flood has seized her eggs
      She comes up now to complain to Sun."

THE END

Printed in Great Britain
by Amazon